Making History

Making History

A Visual Record of the CAW's First 25 Years

Introductory Essay by Ken Lewenza

Foreword by Maude Barlow

National Automobile, Aerospace, Transportation and General Workers Union of Canada

CAW-Canada, August 2010

www.caw.ca

Photo editing and production by Vincenzo Pietropaolo.
Design by David Vereschagin/Quadrat Communications.

Foreword © 2010 by Maude Barlow.
Preface © 2010 by Vincenzo Pietropaolo.
All other texts and interviews © 2010 CAW-Canada.
Photographs are copyright © 2010 by individual
photographers or organizations as listed on page 166.

Every effort has been made to ensure that all references to
individuals and CAW locals are correct.

The publishers welcome any information that will enable
them to rectify in subsequent editions or other future
publications any incorrect references.

Printed and manufactured in Canada by members of the
Communications, Energy and Paperworkers Union of
Canada at Thistle Printing Limited.

Library and Archives Canada Cataloguing in Publication

Lewenza, Ken, 1954–

   Making history : a visual record of the CAW's first 25
years / Ken Lewenza, Peggy Nash; Vincenzo Pietropaolo,
photo editor.

Issued also in French under title: L'histoire en marche.
Includes bibliographical references.
ISBN 978-0-9734185-3-8

   1. CAW-Canada—History—Pictorial works. 2. Automobile
industry workers—Labor unions—Canada—History—
Pictorial works. I. Nash, Peggy, 1951– II. Pietropaolo,
Vincenzo III. CAW-Canada IV. Title.

HD6528.A82C383 2010   331.88'12920971   C2010-904588-2

Contents

Foreword

by Maude Barlow

It is with great pleasure that I welcome you to this special book commemorating the 25th anniversary of the CAW, its history, its accomplishments and its social legacy. I am honoured to introduce you to this volume for many reasons. For one thing, the Council of Canadians celebrates our 25th anniversary this year as well, and like the CAW, is looking eagerly forward to the next 25. As well, Council of Canadians staff are proud CAW members and wear this affiliation with honour.

But most important, the CAW has been a 25-year partner and leader in the quest for justice for workers and others both here in Canada and around the world and its mark is truly inspiring. Born in struggle, the CAW has never wavered from its vision of social unionism, social justice and international solidarity.

Separation from the UAW came as a result of an emerging militancy on the Canadian side of the union in dealing with both concentrated corporate power and government attempts to roll back gains made in earlier times. The courage it took to make this move was forged in the fires of opposition to the unparalleled demands for concessions on both sides of the border, concessions the Canadians were unwilling to make. Several intense years of direct action, plant takeovers and strikes established the tone for a new force in the Canadian labour movement and set it on fire. From day one Bob White and the CAW focused on union democracy, a more unified and militant labour movement and movement building with civil society partners.

This was fortuitous because, at this time, a powerful new social movement was emerging in Canada to oppose the right wing agenda of the Reagan/Mulroney alliance. The first order of business of this unholy alliance was a free trade agenda that would threaten every gain ever made by workers in Canada. Bob White and the brand new Canadian Auto Workers union immediately became a leading force in the fight back and the powerful new coalition that emerged to defend social programs, workers rights and Canada's natural resource heritage. I had the honour of going head to head with Bob against two of the nation's most ardent free traders, Peter Lougheed, then Premier of Alberta and Tom d'Aquino, then head of the Business Council on National Issues – the leading force behind the free trade deals – on a two night debate on CBC national television on the eve of the 1988 election and remember with pride today the arguments we made and the principled stand we took together.

Under the strong leadership of Buzz Hargrove and now Ken Lewenza, our partnership has stayed true and vital. We have walked picket lines together, rolled back pension grabs together, fought for labour justice and human rights in the global South together, and defeated the Multilateral Agreement on Investment – a global investment deal that would have given transnational corporations around the world access to all public spending everywhere – together. We are now partners in a fight to stop the next level of free trade – an assault on sub-national procurement that threatens local wage and labour standards, public services, and local hiring programs. The CAW has been on the forefront of a call to "Buy Canadian" and support jobs and social programs here.

So many things to celebrate this anniversary: the Family Education Centre in Port Elgin, where generations of workers and their families have learned the true meaning of justice and solidarity;

the brilliant research and policy leadership given by Sam Gindin and Jim Stanford; a union that has set the benchmark for bargaining with concentrated power; a powerful voice in building the international labour movement.

So happy 25th anniversary CAW! Your "culture of struggle" has empowered your own members, but far more than that, it has become a model for a movement, a country and a world of justice we seek together.

Preface

by Vincenzo Pietropaolo

As a social documentary photographer, the opportunity to produce a book on the visual history of the first 25 years of the CAW is a rare honour. Photographs are among the most powerful documents we have, and there could be no more appropriate way to celebrate the union's 25th anniversary. This book highlights some of the key events and moments in the CAW's history since its founding in a historic breakaway from its parent international union in 1985.

My relationship with the CAW goes back many years. In 1999 I produced a documentation of the members of the union while at work – on the shop floor, the assembly lines, on trains, ships and airplanes, in fishing boats, in mines, in health care centres – in short in every sector where they worked, focusing on 100 locations across the country. The result was *Canadians at Work*, which the CAW published as a millennium project, and which is one of only a handful of photographic books of workers at work ever made.

This book is an opportunity to build upon that past work, by going one step further. Through 200 photographs made by over 50 photographers, it traces the dual story of the union's founding and growth as one of the largest and most diverse unions in Canada and its passionate fight for social justice in Canada and internationally. This book has therefore stepped outside the confines of workplace, and right onto the convention floors, into seminars and classrooms, into streets and city squares, on picket lines and strikes, and even in faraway places around the world where disaster has struck and help has arrived through the CAW Social Justice Fund, or where members have gone personally to lend a helping hand.

The book offered an opportunity to utilize many pictures taken by members over the years, and I relied both on their personal family collections and the archives of many local unions. The view that generally prevails in the book is through the eyes of the workers and members themselves. Where necessary, especially in the early years of the union's history, I used some pictures from my own archives, as well as those of independent photographers whose work is rooted in the labour movement.

The process of researching the photos was long, circuitous, and challenging. It involved looking at thousands of images, which I did together with the help of retired CAW Communications Director Jim Paré. I sifted through dozens of boxes of historical prints, negatives and slides held in the archives of CAW Locals 444, 222, 112, 27, 302, 195, 200, 2002, 219, and Mine Mill Local 598. I combed the archives at the CAW National Office in Toronto and the TCA-Québec office in Montréal, and relied also on the resources of CAW offices in Newfoundland and Labrador, Nova Scotia, and British Columbia. For more recent images, I relied almost exclusively on digital images made by enthusiastic members who were directly involved in rallies, labour day parades, community events such as barbecues and picnics, strikes, plant occupations, sit-ins, demonstrations and confrontations with police on picket lines.

It was a daunting process due to the sheer number of images involved, but one of the more satisfying experiences was the "re-discovery" by members of photographs that had long been forgotten, or that had not even been known to exist. Many members warmly shared with me their stories of how they found the photographs, how they felt that they had "rescued" a bit of history, and in so doing became part of the collaborative process of creating this book.

The camera is a simple and common instrument, but a remarkable witness of history, for its ability to produce images that constitute documents of irrefutable and credible evidence. The photographer determines what information the camera records, by framing the composition and by deciding the time when to press the shutter. But once images are taken out of context, especially after many years have passed, they are open to different kinds of interpretation. They cannot tell the full story without ambiguity unless they are accompanied by words in the form of detailed captions.

The captions in this book are therefore as important as the images, for one informs the other. In "reading" the images, the reader is helped by the words which provide a wealth of additional information and position the picture in the historical context in which it was made. At the same time, the words in the caption are infused with the emotional appeal that is intrinsic to the image. As a result, there are two distinct lines of narrative in the book – images and words – with the overall effect that they will interact with each other and braid themselves into one single narrative. If the old dictum that a picture is worth 1,000 words is true, then it is equally true that a picture with a meaningful caption is worth infinitely more.

Just as the CAW has gone through a transformation in its first 25 years, so has the world of photography gone through a fundamental change. At the beginning of the union's history, most pictures in the archives were black and white prints, many of which showed the wear and tear of having been handled by many people over time. But in the intervening years, photography became digital and electronic, with far reaching consequences.

Digital photography has opened up a world of unlimited possibilities for individuals to record their own history, and many members of the CAW have taken to photography with enthusiasm and passion.

The proof is in this book. At every event, there are several members with pocket cameras, and increasingly sophisticated professional type cameras.

It has been said that history belongs to those who write it, and members are conscious of the fact that no one else is likely to tell their story in the same way. The media's view of unions is not always accurate, for in the end they usually reflect the point of view of their corporate owners, even if in subtle terms. Through digital photography, workers can take union participation, activism and militancy to a different kind of level. The ease and immediacy with which images can be distributed widely through the internet and its various applications has meant that photography has acquired vast new powers. For example, in the past few years news of uprisings in some countries where the media is severely controlled would not have travelled to the outside world were it not for the diffusion of cell phone images through the internet.

But it is important to remember that the ephemeral nature of the digital image is like a double-edged sword. Since the image exists in cyberspace, it is easy to lose access to it and inadvertently throw it into the cyber dustbin of history. I would therefore encourage all members to spend time to store them properly by archiving them in hard drives, by burning a copy on a CD or DVD, and further, by selecting key images of every project and making prints on paper with relevant information recorded on the back. Would the family album have the same emotional impact on us if the pictures were all digital and stored in a computer?

Photographs also play upon our individual and collective memories. A moment captured is a moment frozen in time, waiting to jog our memories in future years. A story told in photographs and words becomes permanent. All books have a life of their own. I am hopeful that as this book is shared amongst union members, and passed from generation to generation, it becomes a source of enduring pride in the history of the CAW.

Celebrating 25 Years of Progress

by Ken Lewenza

Anniversaries are important in the life of our union. Like stopping, if only for a moment, at a cross roads where past, present and future come together. Anniversaries give us a chance to reflect on our past and the many inspiring lessons from our rich history. They provide an opportunity to celebrate our achievements and the list is very long. And they are a time to reaffirm our commitments to shape the future.

In 2010, we are celebrating our first 25 years. It is not just the fact of 25 years. Many organizations chalk up the years. Many institutions manage to float along with the passage of time. So we are not marking just the passing of the years. Instead we are celebrating the kind of union we have made with these years: our strength and determination, our compassion and our solidarity.

Today the CAW has members all across the country, from small towns to major urban centres. Our members work in nearly every major economic sector.

Our union has crossed old occupational divisions and traditional union boundaries. We bring together industrial workers with service sector workers. Our union links those who work in the public sector with those in the private sector. In our ranks are office workers and production workers, miners and fishers, retail workers, hospitality workers, health care work-

ers, manufacturing workers, transportation workers and skilled trades workers. In 25 years, through mergers and organizing, we have built the CAW into a broad based, dynamic union. Our common bond is that we are all workers. But more important we are union members who come together to unite our strength in the fight for better working conditions and a fair and just society.

In many ways we are a different union today than we were in our early years.

Our geography has changed. The diversity of our membership has broadened. All of these are changes we celebrate. We are a stronger union because of them, a better union, a union more able to take on the challenges of the future.

But just as we celebrate what has changed, we also celebrate what hasn't changed: our culture of militancy, equality and dignity; the fact that our fundamental values and the goals which drive us have remained solid, the bedrock upon which we come together in the CAW.

Our first 25 years have been in the toughest times for workers since the Great Depression. The attack on workers has been persistent. The right has been relentless in pushing back the gains that workers have made. Aggressive employers have tried to impose race-to-the-bottom wages and working conditions. Governments have eroded our social protection, undermined our social programs and have reinvented government as champions of the rich and powerful.

Yet during this turmoil we have represented our members well. We have bargained good collective agreements, at times groundbreaking. We have organized new members. We have forced employers to back down. We have influenced public opinion and we have shaped government policies. But we have done more than all of that. We have refused to accept that our standard of living is the problem. We have rejected an ideology of competitiveness and challenged those whose vision of society is shaped by greed and self-interest. We have argued for progressive agendas instead of politically-motivated agendas. And we have joined our voice and strength with others in our communities who believe a different world is possible. Our history has taught us how important it is to insist that there is an alternative and that we can win it.

In looking at the photographs in this book I am reminded about how often our predictions have been dead on. How our analysis of the consequences has been right on the money. How, too often, our fears are realized. Whether it is the free trade debate or the reform of Unemployment Insurance, the mismanagement of the fisheries or the deregulation of the airlines, the elimination of the Auto Pact or the dismantling of manufacturing, the CAW has been consistently right.

That says a lot about our union's credibility. But there's little comfort in saying, "I told you so." Instead our track record lets us imagine what our country could be like if our ideas and solutions prevailed. How different our country would be if workers' demands for economic and social justice carried the day. And that can renew our energy and strengthen our resolve to keep up this fight.

We have used the last 25 years well. Together we have built a great union, an organization built on principles. We have built a union which vigorously defends our members. We have built an organization

intent on ever involving more and more of our members in the decisions that affect their lives – from the bargaining table to the political arena. And we have built an organization that is bigger than a union, bigger than the labour movement, a union that is part of a broad based social movement.

Our history, in part, is made up of the big events that have shaped us. The initial separation from the UAW, the dramatic confrontations with employers, mass protests against governments, the campaigns we've launched, the demands we mobilize around. The photographs in this book powerfully capture a sampling of those.

And our history is made up of what we do everyday. The friendships we've formed, how we treat each other, the groups we belong to, the causes we take up, the determination and perseverance of our members on picket lines, the acts of solidarity in our communities and across the globe. Those too are seen through the photos.

This collection of photos triggers a flood of memories. However unique the situations captured in the photos, there is also a shared sense about them. Even if we weren't there, we've been there – on picket lines, in marches, in standoffs with the police, in union halls, at bargaining tables and ratification meetings, at picnics and celebrations.

In every page there's a wave of emotions. It is clear how strongly those are etched in the faces of our members. At times it is the stoic resolve of too long on a picket line. Occasionally it's the despair of defeat. But more often, it is the outrage at injustice, the exhilaration of being part of something bigger than ourselves and the joy of making the fight. In our members' faces we see the flush of victory, the hope that things will be different as well as the determination to make them so.

And the photos remind us that every victory we have won, every gain we have made, we've fought hard for. And how fragile those gains are. Every generation of workers stands on the shoulders of those who came before us. But all of our gains will be short term if we don't preserve them and if we're not prepared to help others achieve the same. We will honour those past efforts with greater ones to come.

Photos freeze the moment but they give our thoughts free rein. I can't help but wonder what lies behind the frame. What were the steps that got our members to the moment captured in the photo? How incredible it is that we enter the workplace as employees but emerge as sisters and brothers in the union.

I am inspired when a delegate stands up at CAW or Québec Council and nervously admits to the hundreds of delegates that it's their first time at the microphone. They express feeling less skilled, perhaps less able, than some of the more seasoned delegates but how quickly they demonstrate that what they might lack in confidence they make up for in commitment. It always feels good when they are so warmly acknowledged and welcomed. The photos in this book can't help but bring back some of our own beginnings as union activists, leaders and members. They remind us that the union doesn't just exist to provide services or to get things for its members. Instead a union is how workers come together to fight for and win gains for ourselves and for all workers. In these photos is a clear sense of where our strength comes from. The determination of our members to demand change, their willingness to fight for it, combined with the energy, the enthusiasm and commitment of our leadership and our activists.

When unions are weak, workers are vulnerable. But when unions are strong, our social rights are expanded, our democracy is richer, our society is fairer and our communities are more vibrant.

In our 25th year as we look back, we are together, opening the door to the future. Our heritage is to continue the work of building the union. To find in the past some of the answers to the questions that challenge us and to accept that some of the answers will be brand new. Our goals are clear: to strengthen and expand our union; to make our structures and processes even more inclusive; to turn demographic changes into generational renewal and to help strong locals become stronger. We will organize more members, engage more young workers, and we will keep our retired members active. We will push harder, fight tougher, and be more tireless in our efforts to push back against those with power and privilege and to make real gains for our members. Together with other progressives, we will fight for good jobs, we will push for equality, we will campaign for sustainable development, we will promote an alternative economic system, and we will change the course of history. That's our legacy. That's our future.

The Canadian Auto Workers Union

A Visual Introduction

The Canadian Auto Workers union is one of the largest private sector unions in Canada, with members who work in virtually every economic sector from coast to coast to coast.

The CAW is not only dedicated to fighting for workers rights at the bargaining table, it is equally committed to taking on economic, political and social issues that affect its members and their families in the broader community. Since its Founding Convention in 1985, the CAW has continued to grow through organizing and through mergers with other unions.

Today, the CAW is a diverse organization that bargains agreements in 18 sectors of the economy. Women represent approximately one-third of the total membership, which has increased notably over time. Today, members representing equity seeking groups, including workers of colour, aboriginal workers, workers representing the LGBT community as well as young workers are playing an increasingly prominent role in the union's activities.

The union represents workers in a full range of economic sectors including auto assembly, auto parts, health care and social services, general manufacturing, retail and wholesale, hospitality and gaming, road transportation, air transportation, aerospace, rail transportation, food and beverage, truck and bus, fisheries, mining and smelting, education, vehicle servicing, electrical, shipbuilding and others.

The photos contained in the following pages are from a variety of sources and show the ever increasing diversity of the CAW including almost all parts of Canada and an increasingly complex and varied number of workplaces.

The union is made up of hundreds of local unions that continue to build and change to reflect the needs of this diverse membership.

The regional diversification of the union is reflected in the following nine-page photo essay.

Nova Scotia

Newfoundland and Labrador

MAKING HISTORY

Québec

Ontario

Alberta

British Columbia

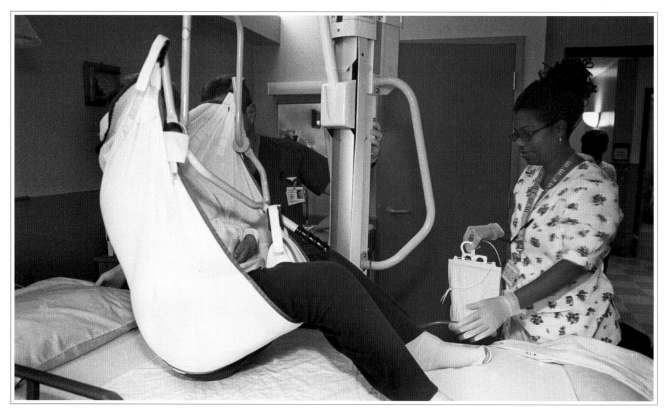

Ontario

Ontario

Ontario

Québec

MAKING HISTORY

Manitoba

Ontario

New Brunswick

Saskatchewan

MAKING HISTORY

Prince Edward Island

Ontario

An Interview with

Robert White

by Randy Ray

Bob White was born in Ireland and came to Canada at age 13. He worked for Hay and Co. in Woodstock, Ont., and by 1959 had become president of UAW Local 636. He was appointed UAW international representative, and in 1964 coordinator of the organizing staff. In 1972 he became assistant to UAW-Canada director Dennis McDermott. White led Canadian members in a 1984–85 secession movement from the American UAW. White was acclaimed the first CAW-Canada president at the Founding Convention for the new union and served three terms. He left the CAW in 1992 when he was elected president of the Canadian Labour Congress, a position to which he was re-elected in 1994 and 1996 and from which he retired in 1999. White served as president of the Trade Union Advisory Committee (TUAC) of the Organization for Economic Cooperation and Development (OECD) and was the chair of the Commonwealth Trade Union Council and of the Human and Trade Union Rights Committee of the International Confederation of Free Trade Unions. He was also vice-president of the New Democratic Party. In 1990 White was appointed an Officer of the Order of Canada. His autobiography, Hard Bargains: My Life on the Line, was published in 1987.

Q: You launched your trade union career at Hay and Company in Woodstock, Ont. in the 1950s as a member of UAW Local 636. Back then, did you ever imagine you'd be involved in the founding of an all-Canadian union for Canadian autoworkers and other workers?

A: I never imagined I'd even belong to a union. We came from Ireland, my dad was working there, at Hay and Company as well, and he said, "Don't get involved in the union, they're all a bunch of communists" … and I got involved.

In 1957 I went to my first ever convention. Walter Reuther, UAW President was speaking. I'd never been to a UAW convention … Walter got up to speak, and it was spellbinding. He was covering world issues; he was covering issues of racism in the United States, the whole problem of blacks having separate washrooms in local unions. It was absolutely fascinating, and from then I started taking a bigger interest in the union, and ultimately ran for president of my local union. I loved it.

When CAW broke away from the UAW, some argued the split would undermine the historic internationalism of progressive unionism. Did the breakaway strengthen the Canadian labour movement?

Ultimately the separation from the UAW strenthened the labour movement here in Canada. Initially though we were concerned about how the corporations would respond. I remember the first call I got after we'd come out of the founding convention was from Roger Smith, the president of General Motors at the time. He said, "Bob, we recognize what you've done and we've got to find a working relationship. I'd like if you could come with your assistants to the General Motors building; I'd like you to have lunch with myself and some of the vice-presidents so you get to know them." There were a lot of people that were nervous . . . were the corporations going to recognize us? Were they going to bargain with us? I didn't have much doubt that they would. We had great support from the activists, great support from the rank and file members of our union.

It was seen in Canada as being an important decision for the Canadian labour movement. A number of international unions didn't like what we did because they thought we were turning our backs on Americans. For us at the time it was very exciting. When you look back at it now, I think it was really a crucial decision for us to make, and we became a much better union as a result.

Wasn't the perception that to be strong, you had to be international?

Yes, as part of forming our own independent union we also made great efforts to establish very good international contacts. We never saw the U.S. as really international; it really was a North American union.

But we played a role in the International Metal Workers Federation and the International Textile, Garment and Leather Workers Federation. We expanded our contacts with other workers around the world so we had our own autonomy; we had our own credentials. We received a number of delegates in Canada, from countries around the world, so we were truly, I think, an international union.

We were Canadian but we cast our vision internationally. I met with the current president of Brazil, Lula, when he was involved in the metal workers union, became good friends with him, we were in Latin America lots of times, and wherever we went our union had good credentials. I know this was because as a union we didn't have a narrow vision of what the labour movement should be, but had a broader vision.

When CAW was born there were fears that the union would be ruled by a few at the top. How did the formation of the CAW Council allay those fears and ensure CAW was a democratic union?

Within the UAW, we had a Canadian Council, but we never had an executive board. Local unions had an executive board but we never had one, so we sat down as a small group: "Look, I said, we're going to have an executive board which will include the Canadian council executive, the president, the secretary-treasurer, as two key positions, their closest assistants would be there with voice but no vote. We were going to have that board and the majority of that board are going to be rank and file local union leaders, who are elected and become council leadership." From the board, what we got was great input, people felt they could participate and reach a collective decision.

Early on the CAW developed a no concessions policy that some people at the time said would lead to closures of workplaces in Canada. How risky was that strategy and what has been the effect of the policy in the past quarter century?

As a result of this important policy, going into negotiations our members weren't scared; they didn't have to run for cover, we weren't going to let employers slash their wages and benefits and stuff like that.

I remember in Brantford, Massey Ferguson was closing plants anyway. At the end of the day, they closed all their plants in Canada… in Brantford, Woodstock, and Toronto. A few concessions wouldn't have helped. We set this policy collectively; we had council meetings, we talked it through with people so there's a sense of solidarity, and the sense that if something was happening and they went on strike then the others would join their picket lines and then we'd be working behind the scenes to try and find the best possible solution. So it wasn't just black and white. We got a lot of decent settlements, and the jobs were saved. But of course then what happens is corporations make decisions regardless of what the union does to move their operations to other parts of the world where they can do business cheaper. Look at Sterling Truck which recently closed in St. Thomas, one of the best operating truck companies in Ontario. Where's it going? It's going to Mexico. It's disgusting.

Which CAW bargaining victories set precedents that spread to other sectors and even other unions?

I think negotiating and improving Paid Education Leave (then as the UAW) and prioritizing equality initiatives were all very important victories for the union. We had full time workers inside the plants dealing with health and safety issues, and human rights issues that fellow workers could go and talk to.

We took these basic priorities into other sectors that we came to represent as a union. The bargaining may look different but our members saw an incredible difference in the way we bargained especially in health care, the way we bargained in the retail sector, the way we bargained in terms of the fishers' union and things like that. They saw that in a very positive light, not just an automatic pattern of how we did it in auto, but a thoughtful approach to how we engage the bargaining committees and how we prepare ourselves and the membership. It's worked very well for most of our people.

The auto parts sector was a big sector that we expanded in and made important headway for our members. I think there was a feeling if the Big Three did well, then there's a chance that other workers in supplier workplaces would do well, too.

What do you consider CAW's most important legacy?

The formation of an independent, progressive Canadian union. I don't think there's any doubt. Without that, we would be a fundamentally different organization today. And that gave us a self-confidence that we could be something better and it gave us an opportunity to really look internationally and be a voice on international issues. It gave us a chance to bring more people in to the organization, be more diverse. It gave us a chance to be more active in the community; it really was what made us the union we are today.

Toronto, December 9, 2008

An Interview with

Bob Nickerson

by Randy Ray

Robert Nickerson, affectionately known as "Nick," was the CAW's first National Secretary-Treasurer. He was born and raised in Halifax, Nova Scotia, but moved to Windsor, Ontario at age 19 in 1955.

He began working at Duplate Canada Ltd., where he joined UAW Local 195 in Windsor. He became a union activist and after the company closed its Windsor plant and moved production to Oakville, Ontario, he helped organize the workers, bringing them into UAW Local 1256.

After serving as a committeeman and chairperson of the plant, he was elected president of Local 1256 in 1964 – and served in that post until 1967, when he joined the staff of the UAW in Canada as an international representative. He serviced UAW locals in the London area, including the members at Northern Telecom.

Appointed assistant to the Canadian Director, he was closely involved in the negotiations to break away from the UAW and create the CAW. Elected National Secretary-Treasurer at the CAW's Founding Convention in 1985, he won re-election at every subsequent convention, and served until he retired in 1992.

Nickerson was an outspoken leader in the push for good pensions and benefits, and full participation for all union members, especially for more women in decision-making positions in the union. He has served in a number of important positions in the labour movement, including vice-president of the Ontario Federation of Labour and chair of the Toronto Occupational Health Clinic. In 1990, he was the Canadian delegate on the international labour mission to observe elections in Nicaragua.

Nick remains active to this day, recently helping to organize the fight for fair pensions for former Northern Telecom workers.

Q: When you joined UAW Local 195 in Windsor, Ontario did you ever imagine you'd be involved in the founding of an all-Canadian union for Canadian autoworkers and others?

A: Never in my life would I have imagined that would have happened. I didn't know the first thing about unions. I came in to the plant right out of eighth grade and got educated very quickly about what the purpose of the union was.

In his book, Bob White paced a lot at night wondering when and if the settlement that the new union had negotiated with the UAW would come. It was the payment for the dues that Canadian members had

contributed to the international union as well as other assets. How significant was it that the cheque finally landed in your hands?

It was very significant. The point that Bob makes in his book is that we kept getting jacked around based on whether or not we were going to use the name the UAW (United Auto Workers) … we had an agreement, by the way, that we would be able to use UAW-Canada. And then UAW President Owen Bieber changed his mind and said, "No you can't use that name because that's our name."

Of course we were very happy once we came up with the CAW, Canadian Auto Workers union … we were happy to get the cheque and once we got the cheque, we were able to make the deposit.

The strike fund had to be guaranteed, our members were concerned about whether or not we would have sufficient funds to be able to continue the kind of bargaining we've traditionally done and be backed up with the strike fund. Also, it was important for our members to see that we did have a substantial amount of money to start up our union, and that the dues money would be going into that. Once we got that cheque and I crossed that border, I breathed a very, very heavy sigh of relief. Let me tell you, I was happy.

You played a key role in the rebuilding of the Family Education Centre in Port

Elgin, Ontario. And there is a room in the building for socializing known as Nick's Place. Why was the expansion of the centre so important to the CAW in your view?

The original education centre was the backbone of the UAW and has become the backbone of the CAW. Without education of our leadership and our rank and file, and developing leadership, you cannot build a strong union. So it was very important for us to go ahead and rebuild the centre, so that we could build the strong union we needed in Canada.

You were one of the male leaders that led the internal fight to establish affirmative action positions on the Ontario Federation of Labour's executive board. What did that mean for CAW women members and other women in Canada's labour movement?

At the point in time, OFL President Cliff Pilkey and the executive board in the Ontario Federation of Labour decided to have a women's committee. I was the first person to put my hand up as the vice-president of the Fed to say that I wanted to help establish a women's committee. I was very happy to be a part of that, and very happy to be a part of assisting the women to make their way within the union movement the same as men have, sharing with them lessons on how to caucus, how to make sure that they were going to get their points across, how to grab the mikes on the floor, how to do all of the political things that were necessary to make sure that they had equal rights and opportunities to the men to participate in the union's structures.

It's been very important for the rank and file women, especially in the CAW. Women are in the plants, at the conferences, at collective bargaining conferences, and at CAW Council. Women leaders started to get a lot stronger and much more visible as a result of our involvement and our position on affirmative action.

Looking at society in general over the past 25 years, can you pinpoint one

particular place where CAW had its most important or significant influence?

In the last 25 years the CAW's significant influence of course was when we set up our own union … that was very important to the labour movement in Canada. And as a result of that, as you can see from the expansion of our union, we were able to bring in a lot of other unions that were looking to have their membership represented by a Canadian union. We have a strong membership that includes other merged unions, like the railways, the airlines, the electrical workers and others. That's helped us to build a very strong union that speaks out on behalf of working people.

Toronto, December 16, 2008

Claude Ducharme

The late Claude Ducharme served as the first CAW/TCA-Québec Director, elected May 26, 1985 after serving four years as the UAW's Québec director.

He first worked as a laboratory technician at a BP Refinery in Anjou, Québec, where he spoke out against injustices faced by workers. He soon became active in the Oil, Chemical and Atomic Workers Union and later joined CUPE. He became part of the UAW in 1971.

Ducharme, who was also a vice-president of the Québec Federation of Labour, passed away suddenly on March 21, 1995 while attending a union convention in Paris, France.

At the funeral, former CAW President Buzz Hargrove paid tribute to Ducharme and his devotion to family, his union and his 'beloved Québec.' In particular, Ducharme's commitment to social struggle, to equality, and working people in Québec and their right to determine their own future was cited.

Ducharme was one of the original board members of the Solidarity Fund, a Québec union-run investment fund. Over his many decades of work in the labour movement, Ducharme advocated many causes on behalf of workers including the need to increase the use of French in the workplace in Québec.

Fernand Daoust, past President of the QFL, said of Ducharme: "In all his actions he consistently defended the vulnerable and affirmed the aspirations of Québec within and outside the trade union movement."

In addition to his commitment to the labour movement, Ducharme was active with the Parti Québecois from its inception. He represented the labour movement on a number of government agencies.

Claude Ducharme is elected a Vice President of the Québec Federation of Labour in 1981. He is hoisted on the shoulders of Richard Gagnon, Secretary-Treasurer of Local 1044, helped by other members of the UAW.

The Birth of the Union

The CAW officially began at the Founding Convention, held on September 4–7, 1985 in Toronto, when delegates adopted a made-in-Canada constitution and a new name, UAW/TUA Canada. The name was subsequently changed at a special convention on June 10, 1986, to CAW/TCA Canada. The full name, later amended to reflect changing circumstances, was *The National Automotive, Aerospace and Agricultural Implement Workers Union of Canada – Syndicat national des travailleurs et travailleuses de l'automobile, de l'aérospatiale, et de l'outillage agricole du Canada*. The new union had collective agreements with about 300 corporations in Canada and approximately 120,000 members.

Right and page 23, top: Bob White addresses Founding Convention; *page 23, bottom:* Ken Gerard, chairperson of the Canadian UAW Council, and Bob Nickerson applaud White's comments.

The Founding Convention was attended by prominent Canadian and international labour and political leaders. *Page 24 top*: Bob White with Louis Laberge of the Québec Federation of Labour; *lower left*: Dennis McDermott, of the Canadian Labour Congress. *Lower right:* Ed Broadbent, of the federal NDP.

Page 25, top: Victor Reuther, a founding leader of the UAW in the United States. *Bottom*: The first National Executive Board of CAW/TCA Canada was made up of rank and file leaders, reflecting a new direction in Canada's labour movement. The picture below shows an early National Executive Board meeting. *Front row, left to right*: Ken Gerard of Local 444; Bob White, National President; Bob Nickerson, Secretary-Treasurer; Claude Ducharme, Québec Director. *Back row*: Gerry Michaud, Local 199; Roxie Baker, Local 1325; Ken Ouellette, Local 1915; Brian Feil, Local 707; Phil Bennett, Local 222; John Bettes, Local 112 ; Jean-Pierre Fortin, Local 510.

Page 26, top: In 1984 Canadian UAW leaders presented Prime Minister Pierre Trudeau with thousands of postcards demanding stronger Canadian content rules for Canada's manufacturing sector. This was the culmination of a national campaign by the union.

Page 26, bottom: Opposition to the Free Trade Agreement was the central theme of the CAW's contingent in the 1987 Toronto Labour Day parade.

Above: On January 2, 1988, workers demonstrated their opposition to Canada-U.S. free trade by closing the world's busiest border crossing, the Ambassador Bridge between Windsor and Detroit.

Left: The first victim of the Free Trade Agreement was the Fleck Manufacturing plant in Centralia, Ontario, which was closed and moved to Mexico. Ten years earlier the women workers of Fleck, with strong backing from locals in the area, had prevailed in a long, bitter strike marked by scabs and police violence. The strike paved the way for Rand Formula legislation in Ontario.

Page 28: Members of Canadian Air Line Employees Association (CALEA) picket Air Canada (*top*) and Pacific Western Airlines (*below*). CALEA merged with the CAW in 1985, becoming the first of many mergers with the union.

Above: Canada's airline industry held its breath as negotiations between the CAW and Air Canada to save Air Canada from bankruptcy went to the 11th hour in May 2004.

CAW President Buzz Hargrove, along with then CAW Local 2002 President Sari Sairanen, announce a tentative settlement with Air Canada. The announcement came after a nine hour meeting convened by Justice Warren Winkler and the Air Canada negotiating team.

In the 1980s, the Canadian Labour Congress established the Union of Bank Workers to address low wages and poor working conditions in the sector, positions predominantly held by a growing number of women entering the workforce. Workers at the Bank of Commerce VISA department in Toronto staged an overnight sit-in, and began a strike that lasted almost nine months. The strikers were mostly women, many of them single parents or immigrants. The CAW took a leading role in this strike, and other initiatives, in an effort to improve women's working conditions.

Above and page 31 top: Members of the Union of Bank Workers celebrate after winning their first collective agreement, 1986.

Page 31, bottom: Bank workers marching at the Bank of Commerce Centre.

During the CAW Founding Convention in September 1985, the entire convention joined the Union of Bank Workers' picket line at the Bank of Commerce Centre in Toronto's financial district. In this photo, Bob White, with Shirley Carr and Dennis McDermott of the CLC lead the demonstration.

The workers at the Unicell plant in Scarborough, Ontario – almost exclusively new Canadians – went on strike in 1988 against an employer who was determined to keep the union out. Their lengthy fight

MAKING HISTORY

galvanized the support of the labour movement, as well as the Ontario NDP both in the Legislature and on the picket line. Their victory became an example for other immigrant workers to stand up for their rights in the workplace. In the photo, a group of workers on the picket line pose with Ontario NDP leader Bob Rae.

In 1987 the CAW made pensions the priority issue in their first round of negotiations with the Big Three as an independent Canadian union. GM and Chrysler threatened to pull out of Canada if the union achieved their demands, but the bully tactics backfired and led to a public outcry. The union targeted Chrysler, and after a three-day strike won the most significant pension improvements ever – large increases up front,

large increases for current retirees, and cost-of-living increases in each year of a three-year agreement.

Above: CAW members on the Chrysler picket line in Windsor.

Page 37: CAW retirees at the 1987 Collective Bargaining Convention lobbying for improved pensions and indexing.

The UAW had agreed to give the new Canadian union $36 million as their share of the strike fund and other union assets, but the final settlement took months to complete. Meanwhile, dues from Canadian locals went into a separate account, and expenses in Canada were paid from the account. By the time the money was handed over it had grown to over $43 million.

Page 39, top: At the CAW's Second Constitutional Convention held in Ottawa in November 1988, Bob White and Bob Nickerson welcome Richard Cashin, President of the Fishermen, Food and Allied Workers Union (FFAW) which had merged with the CAW.

Bottom: Also in attendance were Stephen Lewis, former Leader of the Ontario NDP and former Canadian Ambassador to the UN, and Victor Reuther, one of the founding leaders of the UAW.

Pages 40–41: Bob Nickerson, Ken Gerard, Shirley Carr and Bob White cut the ribbon to officially open the CAW Family Education Centre in Port Elgin, Ontario, October 1, 1988

Above: Canadian Labour Congress President and former UAW Canadian Director Dennis McDermott congratulates CAW President Bob White. *Right:* Victor Reuther, a founding leader of the UAW, in conversation with Sam Gindin, then assistant to the CAW President with his son Jonah, while four young people take a pause from the opening ceremonies (*opposite page*).

The rebuilding of the Port Elgin Family Education Centre was one of the first decisions of the new CAW as a commitment to building a new culture of education, collective deliberation and discussion. The Centre features Canadian materials (Ontario stone and B.C. cedar), state-of-the-art educational technology, and excellent design and construction by union labour integrated into the natural wooded setting. It is the home of the Paid Education Leave (PEL) program negotiated with employers, and the site of many union courses and conferences. The photos on these two pages depict human rights training (*right*), health and safety training and delegates to the 1988 CAW Women's Conference (*page 45*).

Dan Benedict, former International Metalworkers' Federation Assistant General Secretary, and then retired UAW Canadian staff representative, speaks at a CAW event in Québec soon after the formation of the independent Canadian union. (TUA was the French name of the union before the split, and some of the old signs were still being used.)

Page 47, top: Bob White addresses the Québec Council in 1992.

Page 47, bottom: The CAW delegation to a conference of the International Metal Workers Federation. In the front row are Jean-Pierre Fortin (currently the Québec Director), and then Québec Director Claude Ducharme.

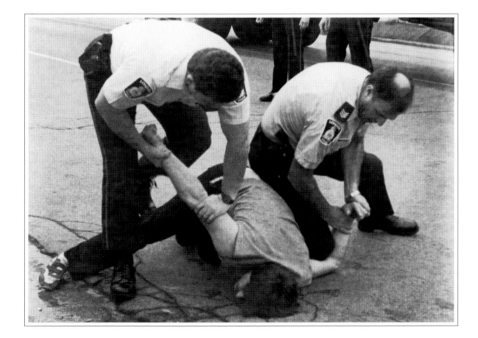

The CAW was in the forefront of many labour and social causes. On page 48 and page 49 (*top*) CAW members rally against legislative changes to Ontario's Workers Compensation Act proposed by the Liberal government in 1989. CAW members came to the support of SEIU Local 220 members involved in a violent strike at Canadian Linen Supply in London, Ontario in 1987. *Left:* In this photo CAW Local 27 activist Cec Devine is wrestled to the ground by police.

The media waits for workers to walk out of the Ford Oakville plant, at midnight September 14, 1990, beginning a 10-day strike.

CAW Maritime locals take part in the Day of Concern, 1991, marching over the Angus L. Macdonald Bridge which links Halifax and Dartmouth.

Page 54 and above: On April 12, 1991 Caterpillar of Canada announced plans to close its Brampton, Ontario assembly plant and move front-end loader production to North Carolina. The Free Trade Agreement set the stage by phasing out penalties for not meeting Candian content standards. The company refused to negotiate a closure agreement until workers staged a six-day occupation. Eventually they forced the company to bargain an improved closure agreement.

Left: Budd Automotive workers block a railroad line during 1991 strike, Kitchener, Ontario.

Federal government mismanagement of the fishery, including inaction against foreign overfishing, has led to the devestation of fishing communities. Here a rally is held in Toronto's Nathan Phillips Square on April 28, 1990 in solidarity with the CAW/FFAW members' efforts to save the fishery.

The road transportation sector is a growing part of the CAW representing more than 20,000 members including truck drivers, couriers, urban/interurban transit workers, armoured car security, taxi and school bus drivers, dispatchers along with a number of other ground passenger office and service workers.

Top: CAW member with bus in Victoria, B.C. in 1999

Left: A CAW long distance truck driver in Sydney, Nova Scotia.

Pages 58–61: Thousands of CAW/FFAW members, their families and supporters gathered in a massive and historic protest against foreign overfishing, in St. John's, on March 29, 1992.

Buzz Hargrove is elected president of the CAW, at the Special Constitutional Convention of June 27, 1992, in Toronto, replacing Bob White who became president of the Canadian Labour Congress.

An Interview with

Buzz Hargrove

by Randy Ray

Buzz Hargrove was born and raised in Bathurst, New Brunswick. He began his union life as a Windsor autoworker and held several in-plant and local executive positions at Local 444 before being appointed to the union's staff in 1975. Three years later, he became the assistant to then UAW Canadian Director Bob White. Hargrove was acclaimed as CAW National President in 1992 and was re-elected every three years until retiring in 2008. While president, he served as the vice-president of the executive committee of the Canadian Labour Congress. Hargrove authored an autobiography entitled Labour of Love: the Fight to Create a More Humane Canada, *in 1998, and* Laying it on the Line: Driving a Hard Bargain in Challenging Times, *in 2009. He was named an officer of the Order of Canada in 2008, and is Distinguished Visiting Professor at Ryerson University.*

He has received honourary doctorates from Brock University, the University of Windsor, Wilfred Laurier University, Ryerson University, the University of New Brunswick and Queen's University. He was also named a Fellow of Centennial College.

Q: During your 16 years as CAW National President, what would you say was CAW's most important influence on Canadian society?

A: I think it's the work we've done on equality and human rights – particularly around violence against women and racism. In the late 1980s and early 1990s when we were still thinking a great deal of what the union should look like and what issues we would take on as a union, we made the decision to embrace this growing diversity and not be afraid of what differentiates us – whether it be race, gender, sexual orientation, religion, language, ability or even geography. There were those in the union that claimed that considering or even focusing on our differences would be damaging to the union and distract it from its core task of defending workers' rights. Many of us didn't believe this argument to be true. In 1991, our convention slogan was "Solidarity in Diversity" which was a bold statement for that time. I think it has shaped our union for the better and allowed us to have a relevant voice on a variety of important social issues. We've had an impact on Canadian society not just because of what binds us as working people, but what makes us different from each other as well.

Over the years, we've also done a great deal of national and international solidarity work. A couple of recent examples are the work of our skilled trades members. We sent a number of our trades people to

New Orleans after Hurricane Katrina to help rebuild some homes. After the success of this project, we collaborated with the Assembly of First Nations to work on some re-building efforts here in Canada. In the community of Little Salmon Carmacks in the Yukon, four years had been spent studying drinking water in First Nations communities that was unsafe – four years, if you can imagine. The First Nations people were forced to boil water because it wasn't safe to drink. Teams of CAW members went to the Yukon in the summer of 2008 and 2009 and now the homes have safe drinking water, on account of the work our members did to refurbish the wells. Who knows how long it would have taken had this community relied on the government to do it – or if the government would have done it at all.

I can say that we've had a major impact on society and on politics more generally in Canada through the actual work we do, leading by example.

CAW's work goes well beyond collective bargaining for union members then?

Oh yes, we are the lead social union in the country, and I believe the lead social union around the world, which means we draw our strength from our members and our families. We take our work into the community, into the provinces, into the country, and internationally on behalf of CAW members and you know what's interesting? I've never had one criticism, I've never had a member e-mail me or call me to complain about this work. Our people support the social work of the union because we bring everyone along.

You've often stated, "the union binds the human family." How has CAW helped pull together the human family in your view?

Quite literally, we do pull together families through our Family Education Centre in Port Elgin where we bring families together every summer from coast to coast to coast through the Family Ed program, and that binds our union together. Members can apply

and come to the centre for the week or two-week program, along with their families so that their spouses and children can learn more about the union and social justice as well.

I believe we get less criticism of the work we do over and above our collective bargaining, the social work we do, the political work we do, because we do bind families together across Canada, families of all different backgrounds. We deal with our issues, we give voice to those who are marginalized, those without power and even give a voice in the halls of power, and that makes a big difference. That's what keeps us together as a union but that also draws great respect from Canadians.

More broadly speaking though is the way that we pull together "the human family" through organizing across sectors and identities. We've made a conscious decision to organize in nearly every sector of the economy, including a number of different non-traditional sectors – so that workers in retail, health care, education, fisheries, hospitality can also be represented by the CAW – which brings us together as working people for the goals of advancing workers' rights and creating a more just society.

Over the years, you as the president, and other CAW officials have often argued that the business communities have tried to isolate labour and block labour from having input. How has the CAW been successful during the 25 years of its existence in helping working people have a voice?

As a union, we constantly challenge the status quo. When employers have closed plants, not paid workers their severance and have not treated them properly, we've occupied those plants, sometimes for days on end, to force them to deal with the issues. We've been the lead union in terms of social protest. When Harris got elected as premier of Ontario in the 1990s and started the cutbacks we were the lead union in starting the Days of Action that shut down a dozen major communities in the province and took people to the streets to demand change. We didn't defeat Harris after his first term, but we sure backed him off on a lot of the right-wing agenda that he had in store for the people of Ontario.

And we've done the same thing across the country. In Newfoundland I recall being in a protest over unemployment insurance benefits being cut for fish plant workers, over the government not doing anything to support fish plant workers, fighting for early retirements when the cod fish were disappearing. We were there on the streets trying to force the government to deal with that … and in the auto sector, we have lobbied, we have demonstrated, because of the lack of government policy to deal with the auto imports that's killing a lot of automotive towns and throwing tens of thousands of autoworkers out of work.

When we're not listened to, we're going to make sure they hear us anyway by going to the streets. During the 2008 Federal election, our union ran a "Give Flaherty the Boot" campaign and we delivered a few thousand boots to Jim Flaherty's office to draw attention to the number of workers who have lost their jobs because of the lack of government action on the auto industry particularly, but manufacturing more generally.

Globalization and the increasing influence of corporations in Canadian public policy is an issue you have opposed for many years. Why has this been a key issue for you and CAW and how has CAW fared in this particular battle?

I would argue globalization has been around for a hundred years, and it's only in the last couple decades that the corporations have used globalization as a tool to undermine the power of unions, to undermine the environmental movement, and forcing everyone to lower their standards and undercut one another, launching *a race to the bottom*, so to speak, that has been horrible for communities and countries around the world.

I have nothing positive to say about the kind of corporate driven globalization that we have experienced over the last 20 years. We made the argument back in the late 1980s, when Brian Mulroney was proposing the free-trade agreement with the United States, that it would undermine job security, environmental rules, the ability of working people to make advancement, even undermine our social programs, and every one of those things has turned out to be true.

One good example is our unemployment insurance benefit. They changed the name to employment insurance although it did not guarantee employment. All it did was change the name and they cut the benefits in half. Now we're in a crisis in our economy, especially manufacturing, and only about 42 per cent of people who lose their job qualify for any benefit at all. That's just one example of the outcome of a corporate-driven globalization.

Do you have one memorable moment that stands out that you'll never forget in your CAW years?

There have been so many of them, but the 1996 strike at General Motors remains vivid for me. We occupied the north plant in Oshawa, and I recall with a great deal of pleasure the support we received from our members. I remember going into Oshawa to tell the members we'd bargained a settlement with GM, the company wasn't going to move the tools and dies out of their plant and their plant would remain open. I was treated like a hero as I walked into Oshawa into the plant. And when I was leaving the plant, there were just thousands of workers that were circulating around the facility. And they were cheering for me and they were yelling my name, but it was the union, it wasn't me. No one individual can do that.

Also the CALEA merger was the first merger that our union had ever concluded, back in '85. That's a real highlight of my time here. And then continuing the battle to take on leaders of the Canadian divisions of U.S.-based unions who weren't treating their members properly. One of them for example fired all its Canadian leadership because they wanted to join a Canadian union. And we took on that fight and we won every vote; we never lost one vote in that period, and we picked up approximately 20,000 members.

But more importantly, we diversified the membership base. We went from a male dominated union, to now where about 35 per cent of the CAW members are women, and the workers of colour make up probably 10–12 per cent of our union. It's been a wonderful exercise and it is great for the union, it'll hold the union in good stead long term as a result, I believe.

If you look back to that day in Detroit and following up in Toronto when the CAW was founded, what would you say over that 25 years would be CAW's most important legacy?

It's the continuation of our commitment to those without power and privilege in our society, our commitment to social unionism.

It would have been easy to turn inward…and say "we have to look after our members, our families, etc." We didn't. We moved shortly thereafter into bargaining with the Big Three, and we had a strike at Chrysler and in this round of negotiations we improved our pensions, we got pension indexing – which was an amazing achievement for our new union.

We carried on our work, our social work…The change was about allowing us to do better in collective bargaining and to play a much larger role in society, both on the social end of it and on the political end of it as well. I can say with confidence that we've done this and will continue to do this long into the future.

Toronto, December 9, 2008.

An Interview with

Jim O'Neil

by Randy Ray

Retired CAW Secretary-Treasurer Jim O'Neil joined the UAW in 1964 while working in the Chrysler Windsor Assembly Plant where he held a number of leadership positions in Local 444. In 1976 he joined the staff of the UAW in Detroit in a servicing position working with the Chrysler plants and offices in Canada and the United States. Four years later he was transferred to the UAW staff in Toronto where he was assigned to the aerospace section of the union and Chrysler. He was involved in major negotiations with Chrysler, General Motors, Ford, McDonnell Douglas and Bombardier/de Havilland. Since the formation of the Canadian Auto Workers union in 1985, O'Neil worked closely with the president's office as a national representative responsible for constitutional matters and appeals from local unions that come before the National Executive Board. He was elected CAW's Secretary-Treasurer in September 1991 and was re-elected every three years. O'Neil was also a member of the executive board of the International Transport Workers' Federation (ITF), which represents more than 600 unions with more than five million transport workers in over 140 countries. He retired in 2009.

Q: You started your career working at a Chrysler plant in Windsor, Ontario as a member of Local 444. Do you have union in your blood ?

A: Yes, my dad worked at Chrysler for 40 years, and my mom was a schoolteacher. My dad worked at the old truck plant right in Windsor, so there's a little bit of union blood there.

The CAW Task Force on Politics was a key initiative in the evolution of the CAW. What was the significance of that CAW project?

Through this initiative we learned to listen. We went out and listened to the membership and the Task

Force, which probably more than anything else, created an opportunity to bring people together.

These were rank and file workers who were pulled out of a lottery of each local, they weren't hand-picked. We didn't know from one day to the next who would show up, and it was a good opportunity to hear what people had to say on political elections. They all said, "You can give us some advice but at the end of the day don't tell us who to vote for, we'll vote for who we think is the best candidate." And I think from that day forward, we've changed a lot of things we've done in our pollitical campaigns. Ultimately, the results of the Task Force have taken us in the direction of strategic voting, and issue-based election campaigns, letting our members decide who's the best, and what's the best for their community.

Where does the creation of the Paid Education Leave (PEL) program and bargaining with employers for funding rank in terms of CAW's accomplishments?

It would have to be one of the top things that we have been able to bargain. I say that because it allows us an opportunity to provide labour education to our leadership and rank and file membership. It gives people an opportunity in the workplace to get away, go to Port Elgin, probably one of the greatest educational centres in the world, and to spend one week, two weeks, up to four weeks, exploring different issues such as what's going on in the country on a social, political and economic level.

How important is it for the rank and file to be well-educated?

Our rank and file members are people that live in the community, they get involved in the community and take this perspective gained from the education back into their community and all other parts of their lives. They have a different perspective, and this gives people a lot of confidence. After taking part in the education program, many members become activists within the union.

The CAW Social Justice Fund derives its funding through bargained money from employers that CAW contributes to various causes such as land mine disposal, digging wells and supporting people whose lives were devastated by disasters. What is the importance of this initiative and where does it rank among CAW's many projects?

The Social Justice Fund and all the hundreds of projects it has supported over the last 20 years is an example of the CAW's social unionism. It's a social unionism that we've practiced. The monies, the projects, give us an exposure outside of Canada and North America, although we do a lot of work within Canada, whether providing support after the ice storm in Québec, or the flooding in Manitoba. But we do so much work to help people in the impoverished countries, whether it's establishing wells for people that have to walk miles and miles for water, or helping with de-mining initiatives. We've managed to de-mine a large portion of Mozambique and children feel a lot safer when they're playing in their backyard like most kids should. Hundreds of mines have been removed so far.

As the union diversified, what were some of the challenges the union faced?

We had to learn from groups we brought in. At that time when I got elected in '91 we had about 115,000 members in the core sectors of auto, auto parts, aerospace, and airlines and then we slowly started learning from others. We merged with other, smaller like-minded unions. We opened up our union, and when I say opened up, we said to them: "You're bringing a different group of workers to us, we have to learn from you." It really changed our union, it brought in a lot more women for example. I guess the largest group would have been the CBRT&GW in 1994 – traditionally men, but it was VIA Rail too, which brought women into our union, and that was about 33,000 members.

And then there were a lot of other smaller mergers... they've all brought different challenges but it's made us a better union, a more diverse union. But we're seeing fewer and fewer workers in auto and aerospace every day. So diversification helped to grow our union. But at the same time we have to look at continuing to expand. Five years ago we had a membership of 255,000 and today it's about 225,000 due to layoffs and closures.

How many agreements does CAW bargain a year and with how many companies?

There's probably today about 1,700 different collective agreements that our staff are responsible for bargaining. When I say that it is not necessarily 1,700 separate employers but it's 1,700 separate agreements.

At the end of the day when you get a deal, what things most affect the future of those you represent?

The key is that when you bargain a collective agreement you have to get your members involved. The bargaining committee has to go to the members, ask them what they want, and then when they do that, some of these demands end up as proposals. You also set a strike deadline. Your members are always involved along the way. They're part of the collective bargaining process. And when you get the agreement you've got to go back to them and get it ratified. From there it makes a difference in their life whether it's more wages, more time off, better working conditions, expanding on healthcare. It not only impacts them as workers but it impacts their family as well.

Can you give me some examples of some breakthroughs in bargaining that you witnessed or were directly involved in?

The time off we've been able to bargain has been critical because it's given our members more time off away from the workplace and created a lot of jobs in the process. Somebody has to be on the job when I'm off for a week. That's been a real plus. We've been able

to bargain some excellent pension agreements, job and income security, especially with the uncertainty right now.

What has CAW accomplished that will help protect its members in these tough times?

We've bargained some good income and job security and restructuring programs. What we've been able to do is encourage the more senior people to leave the workplace, enjoy the leisure time and it saved a lot of younger people their jobs. But it will get tougher if things continue where they are right now, and if there is not the political will to change the direction on trade and other important issues.

In the past 25 years what has been the CAW's most important influence on Canadian society?

We've always been out front. Challenging. We've had the right leadership, whether it was Bob White, Buzz Hargrove, and today Ken Lewenza. They managed to take on the challenges of the day. Outspoken, articulate, charismatic, they gained the public's attention. I mean sometimes people in the public would say, "Yes, but we don't like them," or "They're too loud," but at the same time people can't identify any other union leader. We're out front challenging people and I think putting a lot of things back into the community.

Is there one memorable moment in your 25 years that stands out, that you will never forget?

I've just loved everything I've done, I've been so fortunate. I just thought I'd work at the Chrysler plant for 30 years, retire like everybody else. But I got some very important opportunities. Some people had some confidence in me. It's knowing that, as Secretary-Treasurer, I've played a role and made some decisions that bettered the lives of a lot of our members in our communities. That's what is most memorable.

Toronto, December 16, 2008.

An Interview with

Luc Desnoyers

by Daniel Drolet

Luc Desnoyers was one of the pillars of the Québec branch of the CAW. A native of St-Jérôme, he joined the union in 1971 when he was hired at the Kenworth truck plant in Ste-Thérèse where he was a union steward and local president. He became a UAW Representative in 1981 and later took the position of Assistant to the Québec Director, Claude Ducharme.

Following the sudden death of Ducharme in 1995, Desnoyers became Québec Director, a position he held until 2008. From 1995 to 2008, he also served as vice-president of the Québec Federation of Labour. Shortly after leaving the CAW, Desnoyers was elected a Member of Parliament for the Bloc Québécois in the riding of Rivière-des-Mille-Îles.

Q: What has been the main advantage of the existence of the Conseil québécois [Québec Council] within the CAW, and how have members benefitted?

A: The Québec Council is the best democratic tool we've implemented. It was created in the days of Bob White, the first president of the CAW, and it allows us to hold healthy debates within our organization that advance the cause of workers, move politics forward, move the social-democratic issues of the country and the province forward. The debates held within this council have given us a lot of political influence because we work hard on developing a strong connection between the lunch box and the ballot box.

Every time there's an election, we discuss it at Québec Council… we decide what kind of legislation we want to see implemented, we decide based on the type of government we want to see elected, and what type of influence we can have to advance the cause of workers. So it really is one of the finest tools we have adopted. With it, we have succeeded in bringing CAW delegates in Québec together to work, to build and to join in making demands in the interests of Québec.

How is the labour movement in Québec different from that in the rest of Canada, and how has the CAW dealt with those differences?

I like to say that we're a bit like the French comic book Astérix and Obélix – a small village of Francophones surrounded by 250 million Anglophones, and, on top of that, because of our social-democratic tendencies, we have pushed for things that you don't find in the rest of Canada. One good example is the fact that in Québec, we already have $5 to $7-a-day daycare, but the debate about daycare is still going on in the rest of Canada. We all know that, in today's world, both parents work and we need an effective daycare system to help them make ends meet. Another example is the anti-scab law: Québec was the first province to adopt anti-scab legislation. Ensuring more civilized collective bargaining, employer-union relations and workers' struggles – after all, we have lived through some important strikes, and the one that led to all this was at Pratt & Whitney in 1974.

The CAW has always recognized the unique situation in Québec. How has that translated concretely? And has it been successful?

When you look at the structure of the CAW, you see a democratic structure whose leaders, our current president Ken Lewenza is no exception, have always treated Québec the same way, that is, by recognizing the right of Quebecers to self-determination, which has translated into a large degree of autonomy here in Québec when it comes to deciding what we do and how we do it. So when I look back over the 27 years

I spent in the union, I can see that we have enjoyed incredible recognition on the part of the CAW's social-democratic leaders – people on the left who have enormous respect for Quebecers as well as for Québec workers.

The CAW has grown and today includes a greater number of industries. How has this affected Québec?

I would say that it has had a major impact because … we had an automobile plant, GM, which we no longer have; it disappeared. But we can say today, that it was not the only plant; there are now many others. This is a struggle we have fought both in Québec and across Canada, and we are on the same wavelength in that regard. Yes, the CAW has changed, and that's a good thing. We became a Canadian union in 1985, and we couldn't remain just an automobile union concentrated in Ontario, with no presence in any other province of Canada.

Our first major merger was with the CALEA, the union representing airline employees, with a base in each province. So that allowed us to establish a presence across the country and in Québec, it gave us a foothold in different regions where we didn't necessarily have any members. The same thing happened with the railways. There were the railway workers and the skilled trades people – they are all over Québec, and that allowed us to lay foundations and make a name for ourselves across Québec. Each of the national mergers has brought us enormous advances in Québec and taught us how to do mergers in Québec.

When Alcan workers, for example, decided to join the ranks of the CAW – at the time, we were talking about nearly 5,000 workers in the Saguenay region, where we were not already present. But the two organizations, the FSSA [Federation of Aluminum Unions] and the CAW, had strong ties of solidarity and the same way of working. In fact, we were both vocal in our demands to both governments and employers and intent on ensuring that we were getting the best for our members. Each group that has joined the CAW has contributed something new – new solidarities, new ways of mobilizing members and ensuring an increasingly militant organization – often thanks to the Conseil québécois, which has been an important place to exchange with these newcomers. Today, they are all part of the CAW. They're no longer railway workers or CALEA members – they're CAW members. When they talk, they identify themselves with the CAW.

Which victories won in Québec – labour or political – are most representative of the CAW's philosophy of social unionism?

We've waged so many important battles in Québec. Pratt & Whitney in Longueuil, which was United Aircraft at the time, stands out as one of the biggest in Québec. It had a huge impact on the province and paved the way for the Rand Formula to become law in Québec. With people paying union dues, we didn't have to go around collecting them.

There was the anti-scab law, which put an end to in-fighting on the picket lines, where everything could be destroyed depending on whether the employer used scabs. Socially, those two laws changed Québec in terms of work.

Bargaining tables also come to mind – when we negotiated the Social Justice Fund; that also changed Québec. I could mention the severe flooding in Saguenay, where we donated hundreds of thousands of dollars to support the Red Cross in the region and to assist the citizens and workers affected. And it's not just in the Saguenay Lac-St-Jean region; we also provide help to women's shelters and to food banks – and, as we all know, there's an ever-growing need for these services.

How has the labour movement evolved over the past 25 years, and how has the CAW contributed to this evolution?

When you look at the support systems we had at the beginning, our struggles were important ones, but we didn't always have the right tools or arguments. Today, I can say that the CAW has an

excellent research department. When we arrive at the bargaining table, we already know the employer, we know their weaknesses, we know what type of industry it is, we know what the outlook is like for that industry – so we are able to analyze the negotiating situation and to see how we can go about making important breakthroughs at the bargaining tables. I think that's one of the big differences between the past and today.

In my view, the CAW is a truly progressive organization, because everyone is involved in the decisions. It's not just one person in the organization making the decisions. That's the greatest strength of the CAW.

How has the CAW influenced Québec society? Is there any one thing that stands out?

If I start with René Lévesque's time, when the Québec Director was Robert Dean. Robert Dean was a passionate politician, who served as a minister under René Lévesque when he was elected under the Parti Québécois, and Robert was a very influential member of that cabinet. When he left the union to enter politics, a bit like me, he left with the CAW book under one arm and the QFL book under the other arm, and when he would go to the National Assembly or to cabinet meetings, he brought along with him the progressive ideas that are part of the labour movement.

When you look at the composition of political parties today, well, they're not designed to build a better society. They're designed to build and to give a bit more to those who already have a bit more, ultimately, and to take a bit more out of the pockets of those who have less or who have the least, and to give it to those who are richer, while we should be doing the opposite if we want to build a better society. In Europe, there are countries that have managed to do that. Why shouldn't we be able to do the same thing?

What left the biggest mark on you during your years in the CAW?

I think that, looking back, one of the things that also made a big impression on me in my 27-year career was the loss of the auto industry in Québec. When the GM plant closed in 2001, I swear I had the feeling that we were losing one of the most important industries in Québec, an industry that had had a huge impact on Québec. Because we know that when we have a plant, for each job in an assembly plant, it's the equivalent of seven indirect jobs. In Québec, we sell 400,000 to 450,000 new vehicles a year; that translates into two assembly lines, which means 6,000 jobs in Québec if we had our fair share of that industry. That's one of the struggles I still believe in and I'll continue to fight to have that type of industry here.

When I ran for this job as a Member of Parliament, I said to myself, becoming a Member of Parliament in the federal government – that's where all the big decisions are made. And do you know where I learned that? From my union. Because when I would go to Detroit with Buzz Hargrove and Jim O'Neil, and we would sit down at the Canadian Consulate to discuss the auto industry, on the other side there would be 10 Canadian federal government officials and Ontario lobbyists. But nobody from Québec. And that's why it's important to have someone in Ottawa who is capable of asking questions, who isn't afraid to ask them, and who doesn't have to tow a party line. Because in the Bloc Québécois, we're there to represent Quebecers and to demand that Québec gets its rightful fair share, nothing more, nothing less.

St-Eustache, January 13, 2009

Right: Worker processing smelt in a Lake Erie plant.

Bottom: Workers from the *Coranet* fishing boat at the end of the day's work, in Erieau, Ontario, 1992.

Page 75, top: A CAW Local 195 member who works in the Windsor-Detroit tunnel is struck by a vehicle that crashed through the picket line during a strike in 1991. *Bottom*: Worker at the General Motors van plant in Scarborough, which closed in May 1993.

CAW members rally in protest against cuts to Unemployment Insurance benefits planned by the Conservative government in 1993. In photos above and page 77, bottom, the rally winds its way through the streets of downtown Toronto, while Bob White, president of the Canadian Labour Congress addresses the gathering (*page 77, top right*). A family attends another UI demonstration in Welland, Ontario (*page 77, top left*).

Above: Ken Georgetti is elected president of the Canadian Labour Congress when Bob White retired from the CLC presidency in 1999.

Page 79, top: CAW Secretary-Treasurer Jim O'Neil, CLC President Bob White, and CAW President Buzz Hargrove at a Parliament Hill rally in support of Northern Telecom workers, 1995.

Page 79, bottom: CAW President Bob White, United Farm Workers President Cesar Chavez, and Leo Gerard, National Director of the Canadian division of the United Steel Workers picket a grocery store in support of the California grape workers, 1987.

CLC demonstration for decent jobs, Ottawa,
May 15, 1993.

Above: A mock cemetery to mark job losses was erected on Parliament Hill, as part of the CLC March to Ottawa, May 15, 1993.

Page 83, top: CAW President Buzz Hargrove with author and filmmaker Michael Moore during GM bargaining when the author came to encourage the CAW and to promote his book *Downsize This!* in 1996. *Bottom*: Bags full of mock money used in a protest against bank profits in Vancouver, 1996.

MAKING HISTORY

Mike Harris was elected Premier of Ontario in 1995 and moved quickly to attack workers and the poor. The anti-scab law was ripped up, social programs were on the chopping block, and social assistance was slashed by 21 per cent. The response was an unprecedented series of mass protests and political strikes that hit 11 cities across the province from 1995 to 1998. The Days of Action were led by the labour movement, but built coalitions with community organizations and social activists. The first Day of Action was in London, followed by Hamilton, Waterloo Region, Peterborough, Toronto, Sudbury, Thunder Bay, North Bay, Windsor, St. Catharines, and Kingston.

Above: Workers walk through -30 degree cold to the rallying point in London, December 11, 1995. There were 50,000 demonstrators in the streets and most workplaces were shut down.

Page 84: The Hamilton Days of Action (February 23–24, 1996) built on the success of London.

Left: The Metro Toronto Days of Action (October 25–26, 1996) brought the city to a standstill. Some 250,000 protested, making it the largest political demonstration in Canadian history.

Bird's eye view of the march that was part of the Windsor Days of Action, October 17, 1997.

Women's March Against Poverty, Vancouver, May 1996.

In Toronto CAW Council delegates participated in a moving ceremony on December 6, 1997 in Toronto's Nathan Phillips Square to mark the anniversary of the 1989 Montréal massacre when 14 young women at the École Polytechnique were murdered. The event was also attended by Toronto Mayor Barbara Hall.

Opposite page: CAW members at the 1998 International Women's Day march in Toronto. CAW locals across the country sponsored events marking International Women's Day.

MAKING HISTORY

Above: The International Women's Day rally held at the University of Toronto campus, in 1996, was attended by Peggy Nash, assistant to the CAW president; Cheryl Kryzaniwsky, CAW Council president; and Judy Rebick, past president of the National Action Committee on the Status of Women.

Page 92, top: In 1998, 2,000 women and supporters gathered in the University of Toronto's Convocation Hall in preparation for the International Women's Day march. *Page 92, bottom*: A quilt in celebration of Sisterhood, made collectively by members of CAW Local 27.

"Work Ownership" was the CAW's key demand in 1996 negotiations in order to halt the escalating outsourcing of jobs. A settlement was reached at Chrysler, but for the first time in 40 years the second company refused to meet the pattern, and GM workers were forced to go on strike. GM management tried to break the strike by applying to remove 75 dies and molds from the Oshawa Fabrication plant, so they could keep production going in the U.S. The CAW members responded by organizing a mass occupation of that plant, and GM was forced to capitulate.

Top and bottom: CAW members on the picket line in Windsor.

Page 95, top: Workers occupying the Oshawa Fabrication plant.

Page 95, bottom: Oshawa picket line.

The 1997 strike against PC World in Scarborough, Ontario was long and bitter. Emboldened by the Harris' government's repeal of anti-scab legislation, the management refused to negotiate and demanded major concessions from CAW members who were mostly immigrants and workers of colour. They brought in scabs, obtained injunctions, and ignored a ruling by the Ontario Labour Relations Board that they were not bargaining in good faith. The CAW responded with an occupation backed up by 1,000 supporters from nearby workplaces. The massive police presence failed to intimidate the bargaining unit, and a settlement was negotiated. This success inspired a number of other workplace occupations.

CAW members came from across Ontario to join the picket line in support of PC World strikers in Scarborough, Ontario in 1997. CAW national representative Jerry Dias, currently an Assistant to the National President (*top left*) and Hemi Mitic, Assistant to the National President (*top right*) during the PC World strike.

Top: In 2005, members of the McMaster University Staff Association voted to join the CAW, swelling the ranks of post-secondary education sector workers in the union by over 2,000. In response to the growth of members in the education sector, the CAW renamed its former Technical, Office and Professional (TOP) workers sector council to include Education (now the E-TOP Council) in August, 2007.

Middle: The CAW represents workers at many White Spot and KFC restaurants in British Columbia.

Bottom: Members of Local 4243 struck to win a union shop at the Cheesecake Café in Victoria, B.C.

Members of the
UFAWU-CAW car-
ried out a series of
actions to protest
Alaskan overfishing
of Canadian sockeye
salmon.

Jack Nichol (*on
right side of photo*)
was president of the
United Fishermen and
Allied Workers Union
(UFAWU) from 1977
to 1993. He helped
workers in the west
coast fishing industry
during some of its
most turbulent years.
He died in 2009.

Bottom: A
three-day blockade
of the Alaskan ferry
Malaspina in Prince
Rupert, B.C. captured
the attention of the
international media
and forced the federal
Fisheries Minister to
travel to the northern
fishing community to
address the issue.

Page 101, top:
In 1999 Dan Edwards
and his daughter
Danielle went on
a hunger strike to
protest the depletion
of the Fraser sockeye
salmon fishery.

Page 101, bottom:
Salmon fishers burn
their license appli-
cations in protest,
April 1996, Vancouver.

On September 25, 1998 Toronto's Sky Dome was turned into the country's largest classroom as more than 40,000 students attended the Canadian launch of the Nelson Mandela Children's Fund, attended by Mandela himself. The CAW was one of the sponsors of the fund launch, and pledged to carry on the struggle for a more just and equitable society.

Next page: CAW President Buzz Hargrove and Secretary-Treasurer Jim O'Neil joined South African President Nelson Mandela and his wife Graça Machel.

In 1999 Molson's announced plans to close their plant in Barrie, Ontario and move production to Etobicoke, Ontario. They refused to offer workers the right to follow their jobs, and CAW Local 306 members responded by occupying the facility.

Right: Front page of *The Barrie Examiner*, November 22, 1999.

Below: CAW members on the roof top of the occupied Molson's plant in Barrie.

Above: CAW Locals 112 and 673 launched a campaign in 2007 to protect Bombardier jobs in Toronto, using the theme that manufacturing matters to the community. The campaign was launched in response to fears that hundreds of aerospace jobs could be lost if the employer continued to set up production overseas. CAW Locals 112 and 673 represent more than 3,000 production, skilled trades' and office workers at Bombardier in Toronto.

Left: CAW members demonstrate in support of aerospace jobs on Parliament Hill in November, 1992. More than 500 CAW members rallied in Ottawa against the Mulroney government's refusal to protect Canadian aerospace jobs at the McDonnell Douglas plant in Malton, Ontario. CAW Local 1967 used the demonstration to highlight the need for the federal government to step in to ensure Air Canada purchased aircraft with Canadian content instead of Airbus. At the time the McDonnell Douglas plant in Malton was going through massive layoffs.

The CAW launches its shipbuilding campaign in 1999. CAW/Marine Workers' Federation, the Fédération de la Métallurgie Inc., and the Shipyard General Workers' Federation of British Columbia, joined in alliance with the Shipbuilding Association of Canada to press Ottawa to deal with the attacks by foreign builders on Canada's shipbuilding and ship repair industry. *Right:* CAW members working on a U.S. owned ship in Halifax. *Below:* Buzz Hargrove addresses the media on Parliament Hill as part of the shipbuilding campaign.

On page 107, a contingent of CAW members from Vancouver joined 50,000 other labour and social activists, university students and young people in protest against the World Trade Organization meetings in Seattle, Washington, November 30, 1999.

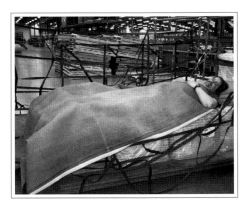

Above and left: On April 15, 1999 CAW Local 1325 members at Johnson Controls in Stratford, Ontario occupy their plant (Can Fab) to protest the company's plan to move their jobs to Mexico. (The plant made seat covers for Chrysler's Bramalea, Ontario assembly plant.) Within a day their fight was won – 57 layoff notices were rescinded and the CAW was guaranteed that the Stratford plant would remain the primary supplier for Bramalea.

Page 108, top: TCA-Québec members protest the closure of rail yards in Montréal. With the merger of the Brotherhood of Railway Carmen of Canada in 1990, and the Canadian Brother-hood of Railway, Transport and General Workers in 1994, the CAW/TCA became the largest industrial union in Québec.

Page 108, bottom: The fight to save the Kenworth plant in Ste-Thérèse was an important battle in Québec labour history. The company announced the "irrevocable closure" of the plant in 1996 after the workers had been on strike eight months. The union shifted its focus to demanding that the provincial and federal governments take action to protect decent paying jobs in Canada. The end result was an agreement between the Québec government, the federal government, and the Québec Federation of Labour's Solidarity Fund to provide new investment and re-open the plant with a CAW contract.

Right and bottom: Members of TCA-Québec join other union activists in Fort Erie, Ontario to protest against the Free Trade Area of the Americas Agreement in a coordinated action with American unions who were protesting on the other side of the Canada-U.S. border in Buffalo, New York. The two groups met in the middle of the International Peace Bridge that links the two cities, April 2001.

Left: On December 10, 2008 TCA-Québec members demonstrate in Trois-Rivières their support for members of CEP/Local 175, who were locked out for more than a year by Petro Canada.

Below: In 1999, about 47,500 Québec nurses were on strike for three weeks. The CAW-TCA supported the nurses in their struggle for better wages and working conditons.

In 2000 the leaders of eight locals of the Washington-based Service Employees International Union (SEIU) approached the CAW with a request to join. This was backed by unanimous votes of the 120 executive board members, and 800 stewards from the locals. Believing that workers should have the democratic right to belong to the union of their choice, the CAW supported the eight locals with the "Taking Charge" campaign. The Canadian Labour Congress (CLC) initially applied full sanctions against the CAW for raiding, sparking a heated debate in the labour movement. A series of workplace votes demonstrated that the vast majority of workers wanted to be CAW members, and eventually there was a settlement between the CLC, CAW and SEIU that involved scheduled votes at the rest of the workplaces overseen by the CLC and Ontario Labour Relations Board (OLRB). The CAW resumed full rights within the CLC and the votes resulted in more than 20,000 new members joining the CAW – predominantly from the health care sector.

Below: Laura Lozanski, former vice-president of SEIU Local 183, and Ken Brown, former SEIU Canadian vice-president, pose after a meeting at the CLC in April 2000, holding the first dues cheque received by the CAW from a former SEIU workplace.

Over 1200 members of Mine Mill/CAW Local 598 waged a tough seven-month strike against Falconbridge in Sudbury, Ontario from August 2000 to February 2001. Despite earning $388 million in profit in 1999, the company demanded concessions, used scabs and spent millions on armed security. The Local 598 watchword was "One Day Longer", and they rallied tremendous support from the local community, across the country and internationally – including a sympathy strike by 350 members of the Norwegian Chemical Workers Union (NKIF Local 40) at a Falconbridge smelter in Norway. The union finally won a new agreement with wage and pension increases. Most of the company's takeaway demands were defeated. The series of images on this page are taken from the video *Mine Mill Fights Back*.

Top: After a tough strike in 2004, 3,600 members of CAW Local 444 at Casino Windsor ratified a new collective agreement by almost 93 per cent. It provided for wage, benefit and pension gains, signing bonuses and other improvements that set the standard for future collective agreements in the gaming industry.

Bottom: Navistar International's heavy truck plant in Chatham, Ontario was the scene of a major confrontation in 2002. Six hundred members of CAW Local 127 went on strike to resist major concessions and fight for the future of the plant. Company use of a strike-breaking security outfit and the attempt to bus in scabs led to clashes. There were serious injuries when a security goon drove over several picketers. Mobilization of CAW members around the province helped win a settlement, but battles over the future of the plant continue to this day.

CAW Economist Jim Stanford (*left*) participates in a panel discussion and debate on auto industry aid at a forum held in Toronto on February 3, 2009. Stanford argued that the uniquely anti-union bent in North American culture and politics is a barrier to the creation of more effective economic policies in key industries like auto.

Below: At a press conference in Toronto's Sheraton Centre Hotel on March 8, 2009 CAW leadership announce a tentative restructuring deal with bankruptcy-bound General Motors (later with Chrysler, and followed by Ford). The deal was part of major restructuring initiative of GM and Chrysler's Canada and U.S. operations that helped secure billions of dollars in government financial loans and which translated into an unprecedented public ownership stake in the two companies. In this photo, from right to left, are Jim O'Neil, Ken Lewenza, Chris Buckley (Local 222), Jim Stanford (CAW Economist) and Peter Kennedy.

In 2001, GM announced the closure of its plant in Ste-Thérèse, Québec. In reaction to that, TCA-Québec members decided to tour across Québec to denounce the closure and government's inaction, especially considering the company had received substantial monies from the government. Led by Québec Director Luc Desnoyers, members of Local 1163 went to city halls in Québec to meet the mayors and councils to tell GM that they cannot take the money from the government and leave Québec without respecting their commitment.

MAKING HISTORY

Right: The streets of Windsor, Ontario were jammed with 35,000 concerned Canadians on May 27, 2007 demanding action from the federal government to protect manufacturing jobs in Canada. Between 2002 and 2007, Canada had lost over 250,000 manufacturing jobs with no meaningful response from government. Representatives from various unions, social justice organizations and community activists rallied to the fight to save Canadian manufacturing jobs.

Below: Canadian Auto Workers union representatives were part of the Canadian Labour Congress delegation at the People's Summit of the Americas Conference, in Argentina, to protest the Summit meeting of the FTAA, the Free Trade Area of the Americas Agreement. Over 30,000 demonstrators marched through the streets of Mar del Plata, on November 4th, 2005, condemning U.S. President Bush and the right wing corporate agenda and demanding human rights.

Top: On May 30, 2007 3,000 labour activists took to Parliament Hill in Ottawa, demanding action to protect manufacturing jobs in Canada. The strong CAW contingent at the CLC demonstration joined members of CUPE, USW, CEP and other unions. The rally was the culmination of three months of forums and actions across the country to raise awareness about the alarming loss of manufacturing jobs. Inside Parliament, members of the CAW and other unions spent the day lobbying members of Parliament from all parties.

The CAW represents thousands of members in Canada's freight and passenger rail industries. (*left*) CAW national and local union leadership in contract negotiations with VIA Rail in 2007. In October of that year the CAW's national "Let's Fund VIA" campaign came to a head when the federal government announced it would inject nearly $700 million in support of long overdue capital funding projects for Canada's passenger rail service.

On June 3, 2008 GM announced plans to close the Oshawa Truck Plant, violating their promise to keep it open that was given in a contract signed less than three weeks before. Furious CAW members responded by blockading GM's headquarters building. Hundreds of people maintained the blockade for the next 12 days. On July 12 thousands of CAW members marched in solidarity past the GM car and truck plants, joined by members of other unions, community organizations, and people from the community.

Top: Blockade of GM Canada headquarters by members of CAW Local 222 at 5:20 a.m. June 4, 2008.

Page 121 top: Chris Buckley, President of CAW Local 222 addresses the blockade.

Page 121, bottom: CAW President Buzz Hargrove addresses the solidarity rally on June 12, 2008.

Solidarity march in support of CAW Local 222
members, Oshawa, June 12, 2008.

The CAW is one of seven unions comprising the Nova Scotia Coalition of Health Care Unions. In October 2007 they embarked on a province-wide campaign to stop legislation proposed by the Conservative government that would take away the right to strike from health sector workers. In the photo above, CAW activists are rallying in Halifax. As an active participant in the Ontario Health Coalition, the CAW participates in coalition demonstrations in Windsor (*page 125, above*) and Toronto (*page 125, below*).

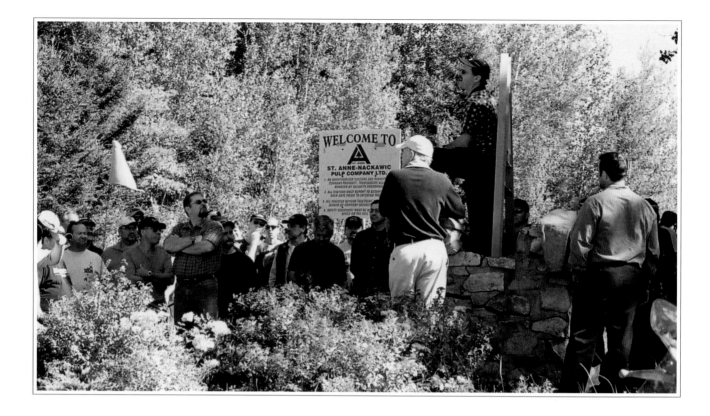

In September 2004, the St. Anne-Nackawic pulp mill declared bankruptcy and closed. They abandoned 400 members of CAW Local 219, their families, the community, and pensioners in the small community of Nackawic, New Brunswick. Immediately following the announcement, some Local 219 members spent the night in the mill in order to prevent anything from being removed, which would affect the potential restart of the operation.

CAW Local 219 organized the community to garner political support for government involvement in order to get the plant re-opened. The CAW worked with the government of New Brunswick to find a new owner for the plant, which re-opened on June 15, 2006 with a reduced work force.

Above: CAW Local 219 President Barry Elsliger addresses a rally of workers blocking the main entrance to the mill, September 15, 2004.

Right and page 127: Rally for Hope, held at the "Big Axe", Nackawic, September 25, 2004.

National and international leaders often address CAW gatherings. *Above*: Phil Fontaine, Assembly of First Nations National Chief addresses the CAW Special Convention held in Toronto on September 6, 2008. On page 128 (*top*), Prime Minister Paul Martin addresses CAW Council meeting on December 5, 2005 in Toronto. (*Bottom*) International Metalworkers Federation (IMF) General Secretary Marcello Malentacchi speaks to CAW delegates at the union's 8th Constitutional Convention in Vancouver, August 2006. Over the years, the CAW has played an active role in the work of the IMF and many other global union federations, including the International Transport Workers' Federation (ITF), the International Union of Food, Agricultural, Hotel, Restaurant, Catering, Tobacco and Allied Workers' Associations (IUF) and Union Network International (UNI).

The CAW Social Justice Fund reflects the union's commitment to social unionism and international solidarity. It is union-controlled, and funded by employer contributions established in bargaining. Since first being negotiated in 1990, it has provided humanitarian aid to projects around the world such as those shown on pages 130–133.

Page 130, top: CAW delegation touring a de-mining site in Inhambane, Mozambique. The project to eliminate land mines is one of many assistance projects funded by the SJF in Mozambique.

Page 130, bottom: This bicycle ambulance in Mozambique was purchased with help from the Social Justice Fund, which helps fund COCAMO (Co-operation Canada Mozambique), an organization on which the CAW is represented on the Board, and which focuses with local partners on microfinance programs for low income women, maternal health/infant health, AIDS/malaria advocacy and homecare for the ill.

Page 131 top: In 2007, Hurricane Katrina left many neighborhoods in New Orleans looking like this.

Page 131, bottom: Lynn and Albert Evans with some of the CAW volunteers who helped rebuild their house in the 9th Ward, New Orleans.

Opposite page: CAW skilled trades volunteers helped refurbish 57 wells in the Little Salmon Carmacks community, Yukon, in 2008–2009. The federal government had failed to do anything to provide safe water despite the community being on a boil water advisory for over three years.

Page 133, top: The SJF sponsors a women's seed regeneration project in India.

Page 133, bottom: CAW members from different parts of the country rushed to provide assistance when a severe ice storm hit the Montréal area in 1998.

Past president
Buzz Hargrove
and founding
president Bob
White congratu-
late newly elected
president Ken
Lewenza at the
Special Conven-
tion of Septem-
ber 6, 2008 in
Toronto.

On October 6, 2008 CAW members and activists from across Ontario joined in the "Give Flaherty The Boot" campaign. To protest the federal government's inaction in the loss of manufacturing jobs, thousands of old work boots were collected and dumped in front of Finance Minister Jim Flaherty's office in Whitby, Ontario. Each boot was tagged with a sign that read:

"Dear Mr. Flaherty
Here are my well used boots. I thought they may be of better use to you, since you have made sure that I will never have a need for them again.
P.S. Sorry I couldn't remove the blood, sweat and tears from them."

Top and bottom: Workers occupied the Aradco Management Ltd. auto parts plant in Windsor, Ontario on March 17, 2009 to prevent Chrysler from removing parts and tooling until workers received termination and severance pay. Chrysler had abruptly cancelled contracts with Aradco and Aramco (its sister facility) forcing their closure. CAW Local 195, representing workers at both plants, used the occupation, a blockade and a rally to win an agreement that provided a significant portion of what the workers were owed. In the photo below, workers gather on the rooftop of the Aradco facility and acknowledge supporters at street level following news that a settlement had been reached, ending the occupation. Workers were joined by Gerry Farnham, Local 195 President (second from left), and Jerry Dias, Assistant to the National President (third from left).

July 1, 2008 was a bitter Canada Day for 2,400 workers at Progressive Moulded Products (PMP) in Vaughan, Ontario. PMP had been Vaughan's third largest employer when it abruptly declared bankruptcy and closed 11 plants. The workers, mostly immigrants, were denied severance pay because bankruptcy laws put workers behind other creditors. Even though they did not belong to a union, the CAW helped set up an action centre for the PMP workers offering support for job searches, retraining, EI and counseling.

In the photo above, some of the former PMP workers take their demands for severance pay to the Legislative Building at Queen's Park, Toronto, March 25, 2009.

Right: Tim Carrie, president of CAW Local 27, and CAW Council president, addresses CAW Council.

Left: The CAW's campaign to ensure hundreds of new Toronto transit vehicles will be "Made-in-Canada" was the cornerstone message in a speech by CAW Assistant to the President Bob Chernecki during a 2008 Labour Day rally outside Toronto City Hall.

Below: The "Made in Canada Matters" campaign was kicked off in 2006 in order to bring attention to the escalating loss of Canadian manufacturing jobs.

Twenty-five years later…

by Peggy Nash

Who could have imagined, 25 years ago, that the newly formed Canadian Auto Workers union would one day become a union representing workers in nearly every sector of the economy – from health care to retail, from fisheries to women's shelters, from rail to airlines to shipbuilding, from cemetery workers to air traffic controllers, and yes, autoworkers?

Who could have imagined that we would grow from being a union with just over 10 percent women to a union where over one third of our members are women? A union that represents workers not just in the industrial heartland, but in coastal communities, mining towns, the prairies, the mountains, small towns, large cities, the east, the west, and the north.

Who could have imagined we would become a union that would stand at the forefront of the fight for equal marriage, gun control, reproductive choice and pay equity? Or that we would play a strong role in breaking the silence on violence against women? That we would one day negotiate Women's Advocates in over 150 collective agreements across the country, ensuring that women who experience violence are protected at work and find access to the services they need? That we would one day succeed in gaining legislation making employers responsible for violence in the workplace? That we would negotiate same-sex benefits contract by contract by contract until it became law throughout the land, in every workplace?

In the last 25 years, we've accomplished many feats that few, at the onset, could have imagined – all with the goal of bringing about greater social and economic equality. Twenty years ago, we created the Social Justice Fund that connected Canadian workers with workers all over the globe fighting for dignity, workers' rights and an end to the crushing poverty imposed by the World Bank, the International Monetary Fund and unfair 'free' trade deals.

Since our founding we have become a union that joins in partnership with Aboriginal communities fighting for land rights, demands an end to massive poverty among many First Nations communities, builds wells to provide safe drinking water where governments have failed to deliver even basic services, and stands in solidarity with Aboriginal peoples in their home communities against racism and hate.

We have negotiated employment equity to force employers to stop racist hiring practices and developed union conferences and courses directly aimed at addressing barriers within the union so we could grow the ranks of worker of colour leadership. We are now also proud participants in the Asian Canadian Labour Alliance, the Congress of Black

Trade Unionists and the newly formed Latin American Trade Union Coalition. We participate in forums and actions that bring the union into communities like the Jane-Finch corridor and St. Jamestown in Toronto and Filipino neighbourhoods in Winnipeg, Muslim communities in Brampton, and Indo-Canadian communities in New Westminster.

We have also negotiated employment equity provisions requiring employers to hire workers with disabilities (who also need to feed their families), and we have won legal decisions forcing employers to accommodate workers with disabilities. We have offered education programs accessible to our deaf members, and some CAW local unions offer sign language training for co-workers and family members of deaf workers so that we can all better communicate.

The union has worked with the No One is Illegal campaign in Toronto and Montréal to stop deportations of undocumented workers. We've campaigned for the rights of temporary foreign workers in hotels, homes, processing plants, farms and oilfields – at the same time demanding exploitative migrant labour policies be replaced with real workplace rights and fair immigration opportunities for workers. And local unions have become hosts to families of trade union refugees fleeing repressive regimes.

Becoming who we are today wasn't accidental. These outcomes did, in fact, begin with dreams and vision. They came about because activists, caucuses, educators and leaders within the union pushed hard to make them happen. They are the result of internal and external struggles, debates, and challenges. We have pushed ourselves to take bold steps, face difficulties, change our culture, and grow a collective vision.

Who we are today follows on clear traditions we had established within the UAW, emboldened by our move to create our own union – a union whose founding constitution called on its officers to embrace equality in ways we had never before articulated. A union that from its outset, recognized that we were, in some ways, two unions – a Québec union and a Canadian union – and that we needed to acknowledge

Confronting homophobia

CAW Local 222's Pride Caucus began in 2002, and in early 2003 activists and top leadership from the local took part in our one-day Confronting Homophobia course, sending a strong signal to members that this was an important issue.

Then, in the spring of 2003, Marc Hall, a Catholic high school student from Oshawa, was denied the right to bring his boyfriend to the prom. Through the Pride Caucus, the union got involved to defend Marc's human rights. The top leadership spoke out publicly on Marc's case, and CAW members came out to the courthouse and the school board to show solidarity with the teen.

Some of our members were angry about the union's involvement, but the leadership stood strong. They were rewarded – not only did Marc get to attend his prom, but the CAW was viewed in a new light by the LGBT community – with many Local 222 members coming forward to say that for the first time they truly felt part of their union.

and respect differences, so we could work strongly together.

Perhaps, in a way, we have come of age. It is a good time to reflect. How has the last 25 years changed how we see ourselves, and even what we do? What does it mean to be a general workers union? How does it change our priorities and our structures? What have we learned from representing such a varied workforce? What are we learning as we become a union that represents so many more women? How are changing demographics affecting how we deal with racism in the workplace, society, the union?

What can we imagine for the next 10 years, or 25? What will it take to get there? What progress will we say we've made on equity issues and worker's rights? Will we have held the line on the gains we've made? Will the women's movement regain momentum in response to the current Conservative government's attempt to strip away our rights? Will we have won a fair immigration policy and stemmed the tide of exploiting temporary foreign workers? Will lesbian, gay, bisexual and trans people feel safer and stronger in our union? When the population of our major cities becomes majority people of colour, will the leadership and membership in our union reflect this massive shift? Will we weather the current economic crisis by standing up for greater social equality, demanding rights for Aboriginal peoples and people in poverty? Will we keep our focus on raising the minimum wage, demanding social housing, and fighting for good jobs for all? How will we have used our sectoral diversity to broaden working class struggle and consciousness? Will our membership be younger, or older?

It's not just about imagining – it never has been. It's about rolling up our sleeves and digging in. Having good, strong debates and challenging ourselves to think critically and to act strategically – with vision. We can be proud of the last 25 years, and put our accomplishments and traditions to use in ensuring that we live up to the awesome responsibility of even more fully becoming who we are.

On March 30, 2007, workers took over the Scarborough, Ontario auto parts facility of Collins and Aikman. The dramatic plant occupation prevented the company from taking out the equipment they needed to shift production elsewhere. The company had no intention to pay the $6 million in severance and other benefits they had promised earlier. The members of CAW Local 303 were backed by solidarity from workers at Collins and Aikman plants in Guelph and Ingersoll, and support from many other CAW members.

The occupation and support was sufficient to force Chrysler, Ford and GM to guarantee the $6 million up front (the plant produced dashboard components for all three companies). It also sparked a series of plant occupations and militant actions by CAW members in defence of workers' severance pay.

The first CAW Pride caucuses were formed in 1990, and the union has since been in the forefront of lesbian, gay, bisexual, and trans (LGBT) issues. Here, CAW activists and allies participate in PRIDE parades.

On October 23–26, 2009 a delegation of young CAW members joined more than 1,000 young Canadians gathered in Ottawa for a landmark conference – Power Shift Canada, the largest ever single gathering of youth on climate in Canadian history. The event was organized by the Canadian Youth Climate Coalition, of which the CAW is a founding member.

Top: CAW President Buzz Hargrove and Québec Director Luc Desnoyers welcome Bloc Québécois leader Gilles Duceppe to the 2004 CAW/TCA Joint Council in Montréal.

Middle: CAW President Ken Lewenza with NDP leader Jack Layton and Liberal leader Stéphane Dion at the CAW Council meeting, December 2008 in Toronto. At the time, the two political leaders were attempting to form a coalition government.

Bottom: The CAW supported the attempt to form a historic coalition government by the Liberal and New Democratic parties, with the support of the Bloc Québécois, in December 2008.

Above: Delegates to the CAW's 9th Constitutional Convention in Québec City, August 2009, elect a new leadership slate. From left: Peter Kennedy, Secretary-Treasurer; Ken Lewenza, President; and Jean-Pierre Fortin, Québec Director.

Left: The National Executive Board, 2010. Front Row: Marcel Rondeau TCA-Québec Council President; Nancy McMurphy, Local 302; Leslie Dias, Local 2002; Ken Lewenza; and Jean-Pierre Fortin. Second Row: Rick LaPorte, Local 444; Tim Carrie, Local 27; Peter Kennedy; and Jean Van Vliet, Local 3000. Third Row: Greg Burton, Local 303. Back Row: Roland Kiehne, Local 112; Chris Buckley, Local 222; and David Cassidy, National Skilled Trades Council. Three other members are not in the photo: Earle McCurdy, CAW/FFAW; Christine Connor, Local 414; and Len Harrison, CAW Retired Workers' Advisory Executive.

An Interview with

Ken Lewenza

by Randy Ray

Ken Lewenza was born and raised in Windsor, Ontario and in 2008 was the first rank-and-file leader to be elected CAW National President. He was re-elected president at the 9th Constitutional Convention held in August, 2009.

Ken is a rank-and-file leader and activist who has emphasized outreach within the labour movement and the broader community during his tenure as a CAW leader.

He began working at Chrysler Canada in 1972 at the age of 18. In 1978, Ken was elected as a steward in the chassis division where his strong desire to improve the quality of life for workers emerged.

Ken held the positions of steward, committeeperson, chairperson and vice-president before taking on the role of Local 444 President in 1994.

He has an extensive background in bargaining including presiding over the first contract with Casino

Windsor and as Chair of the CAW Chrysler Master Bargaining Committee for five rounds of Big Three bargaining. He was also a CAW National Executive Board member and the president of CAW Council for 10 years.

Ken has been involved with many community organizations including the Motor City Credit Union, Guardian Board of Windsor, the labour-sponsored Community Development Group, Hotel Dieu Hospital Board, the AIDS Committee of Windsor and United Way of Windsor-Essex County, in addition to the Windsor and District Labour Council.

In 2002, as a tribute to his hard work and dedication, Ken was awarded the Charles E. Brooks Labour Community Award, a joint initiative of the United Way and the Windsor and District Labour Council.

He is presently a vice-president of the Canadian Labour Congress.

Q: Describe the challenge of leading a major trade union in these tough times.

A: The challenges are obvious. We are still in an economic crisis unrivalled since the Great Depression. Workers are losing their jobs, we face aggressive employers at the bargaining table, labour laws are stacked against us. But even in tough times we make

an incredible difference in peoples' lives. Everyday, it seems, there's another crisis and that makes workers vulnerable and insecure. But the union gives our members a way to fight back.

Keeping the confidence up in people is critical. When you're out there defending the interest of our members, that's how we can continue to be strong.

What in your view should government do to mitigate the impact of the loss of all these manufacturing jobs and other jobs?

The first thing the government can do is stand up for manufacturing and recognize its importance to our economy. The federal government is the cheerleader for the banking sector and the oil companies but ignores manufacturing. Actually it's worse than ignoring. Our manufacturing sector is in trouble because of the wrong set of government policies. We've been arguing for over 20 years now the question of fair trade versus free trade. There's absolutely no question that the job losses in the manufacturing sector and in particular in the auto industry are directly related to unfair trade.

Protecting our manufacturing jobs is critical to our future economic development. So we need to regulate the level of the Canadian dollar, we need to put restrictions on unfair imports, we need to upgrade our plants and equipment and invest in sustainable technologies and we need to limit the authority of companies to close up shop and destroy jobs as they search for the cheapest possible labour costs.

What's the impact of the dramatic loss of manufacturing jobs on your union?

We're a smaller union today as a result of the job loss. We've lost in excess of 25,000 members in a few short years. These are good paying jobs. Without them our communities are in trouble.

When you take a look at the communities of Windsor, Oshawa, St. Catharines, Kitchener, where unemployment is in double digits, it's been devastating.

When we lose those jobs it hits us hard. It's true we have lost dues, but even more, we've lost friends, great leaders and local activists and solid union members. They're hard to replace.

The financial impact of the job loss would be worse if we hadn't become a more diversified union,

geographically and sectorally. The mergers that we've had and the organizing we've done have made us stronger and more able to weather these tough times.

Looking ahead, we face a period of restricted finances in the union so we have to change how we do things. We won't compromise our programs or our commitments to social unionism, so that means we have to build more capacity at all levels of our union to get things done. Our union's strength has never been about money, it's been our values and our determination to represent our members.

It's certainly not the first time CAW's been affected by tough times and bounced back. How will CAW rebound this time?

Unions are fragile. There are no guarantees that a union that is around today will be here in the future. Unfortunately, looking around the world, we have seen once strong and dynamic unions lose their way, and their influence and power.

That won't happen in the CAW. Our union continues to resist and push ahead. And we're not about to let setbacks stop us. Every day our union is fighting and there are wins both in bargaining and in politics. We're still negotiating gains in many of our collective agreements. We're holding the line in others. And where we've been forced to make sacrifices we're determined to make up the lost ground in the future. We've seen our union's campaigns - from EI, to severance and pensions, from local procurement to industrial support for various sectors, from health care to the fight against precarious work - get broader public support. And we've forced government to start paying attention to workers.

It's not a case of bouncing back. It's about maintaining the same culture that we established 25 years ago. It's about demanding a different set of economic priorities. It's about building even more union consciousness among our members and about reaching out more effectively into our communities. It's about organizing new members and engaging more of our existing members. And I think it is about recognizing that no matter how strong individual unions are, our future is at risk, unless the union movement is growing.

Is there a particular strategy CAW will use to negotiate the best possible deals?

I think our strength is in part, our reputation and our resistance to employer demands and attacks. Employers try to keep workers insecure and constantly threatened. After three decades of right wing policies bargaining power is grossly unbalanced. Employers, it seems, have all the cards.

At times we can be forced to do things. The government forced us to re-enter collective bargaining with the Big Three in 2009. Government said, if you're not going to change your contract then we're not going to support the industry, and we needed government support at that particular time.

Today in some sectors we are spending more of our time resisting concessions and rollbacks. But that doesn't change our determination to push for higher wages, better pensions, more job security, improved working conditions and more respect and dignity at work. Collective bargaining isn't just about one round of bargaining. It's about making progress over time.

Workers have the right to expect more and we have a responsibility to build the confidence of our members to actually achieve it. But we also know that we have to do more to ensure that all workers are making progress. Workers make progress in two ways. What we do at the bargaining table and what we do on the social wage front. Our standard of living is not only what we've negotiated from our employers but what we win from government. Raising the minimum wage, increasing the CPP, providing child care support, improving health care coverage, all of those are part of how we make progress, not only for our members, but for all workers.

What changes do you think are needed to protect pensions through legislation to ensure they remain intact?

This will be one of the most significant challenges we face. Any place that has a private pension plan, a defined pension plan, a bargained pension plan, has been threatened in the last year. The global financial crisis put workers at Air Canada in the same boat as workers at the Big Three, and other major manufacturers.

We've had some great success in protecting and maintaining our pension plans. But we've had to fight hard to achieve it. It's outrageous. Executive compensation levels are obscene but workers are told first that we can't earn a decent wage and then we're told we can't get a decent pension. Our pension campaign plans to change that.

In addition to protecting our negotiated plans, we are fighting to strengthen the public plans. That helps our members, but when you recognize that about 70 per cent of Canadians rely solely on a government plan, then it helps millions of other workers as well. We've got to bring everybody up, no one can be left in isolation.

We're going to continue to bargain pension plans, we're going to demand legislation that protects our pensions. and we're going to push even harder for justice for all retirees.

Give me just a few comments on what the next 25 years are going to bring?

We are going to continue the traditions of the last 25 years. We are going to continue to build a strong and dynamic union. And we are going to use that strength to push for social and economic justice.

There's going to be opportunities for unions to expand their membership base because the aggressive demands by employers are not going to let up.

And I think we'll see a more united labour movement. There will continue to be different national unions, and international unions, but I think you're going to see the collective strength of the labour movement come together. And I think there will be more mergers; you're going to see more organizations coming together as one to protect and advance the interests of our members and Canadians more generally.

I think we are at a critical time in our history. For the last 25 years we've kept alive the notion that workers deserve better, that our communities can be stronger, that our economy can be different. I think we are now at a turning point. Where what we do over the next number of years will be incredibly influential in defining what's possible for the future.

We are at a time when an economic system that privatizes profits and socializes costs should be in retreat – when the policies of the right have been discredited and corrupt bankers and corporate bosses are no longer held in such high esteem.

The challenge now is to seize the opportunity. To mobilize our members and to work with other progressive groups to demand the changes we need. I'm convinced that the CAW will lead, inspire and build the confidence in workers to achieve great things.

Toronto, November 26, 2009

An Interview with

Peter Kennedy

by Randy Ray

Peter Kennedy was elected National Secretary-Treasurer of the CAW at the 9th Constitutional Convention in 2009. Kennedy began his career in the labour movement in 1972, after he started working at 3M Canada in London, Ontario and became a member of Local 27. He held various elected positions in the plant and in the local union executive, and has been actively involved in the community as a founding member of the London Unemployed Help Centre, board member of the United Way of London, Art for AIDS, Kids for Kids and the Ontario Aerospace Council (labour chair).

Peter was also campaign manager and organizer for federal and provincial NDP candidates in Ontario and Nova Scotia. He joined the staff of the union in 1989 as director of the education department. He became assistant to the National Secretary-Treasurer Jim O'Neil in 1992, a post that he held for 17 years, during which he oversaw the daily operations of the union, retiree programs, staff relations, as well as collective bargaining with General Motors, CAMI (then GM-Suzuki joint venture in Ingersoll, Ontario) and the aerospace and electronics sectors of the union.

Q: How does government fit into efforts to mitigate the impact of the loss of all these jobs during the recent downturn?

A: During the economic crisis, some have disputed whether government has a role in the economy. Government has a fundamental role to play in shaping our economy and if government isn't there at the end of the day to support and provide assistance to those that elect them, then what is the purpose of government quite frankly? We've seen the manufacturing base in the country virtually disappear, and I've never understood this sort of notion that somehow good paying jobs in the community are bad for the economy, and this gets back to the false notion that workers are to blame for the difficulties that our employers find themselves in. It's absolute nonsense.

The money that is earned by workers regardless of where they work and regardless of the community they live in, is money that's spent in the community. It doesn't go to Swiss bank accounts, it doesn't go to the Cayman Islands, it helps to support everybody else in the community. I've never been able to understand that somehow it's viewed as bad or at least used as a weapon to keep workers down and to minimize their gains.

Is the union worried that it's going to have trouble organizing new groups of workers who might see you as a weakened union?

If you look at our record there's no doubt in my mind if I were out today seeking a union to join, which union I'd be going to. That's CAW. Over the past decades the whole makeup and nature of the union has changed with mergers, not only sectorally with restructuring and manufacturing in auto and the branching out into other sectors of the economy, but in terms of the demographic diversification of the union itself.

We're much more a union of women and workers of colour than we were back in 1985 and those are two of the fastest growing demographics in the workforce. As long as we're doing the things relevant to them, I think we'll continue to be the union of choice for unorganized workers.

How important is it that the union diversifies?

It's fundamentally important. When we separated from the UAW back in 1985 we had 110 to 120,000 members basically in a corridor from Windsor to Montréal, primarily in auto and in auto parts. We've gone from that scenario to today where we've lost 25–30,000 jobs but we're still incredibly strong in terms of members.

Instead of being the predominant union in one or two sectors in the economy, we're the predominant union in 12 or 13 sectors. We've changed the face of

the union in terms of women and workers of colour and ethnic groups and you know we have to continue to do that. We all know and recognize and appreciate that the world is changing. You can't look at the future, without sort of looking at the past. You can't get to where you want to go without knowing where you came from, and that's how I view the challenges going forward.

Certain things are fundamental in people's lives, you know. Education. Health care. Quality of life after having worked and supported the system and provided all of the things that goes into that for 30 or 40 years. The fact is that companies have gone to the brink of bankruptcy and defined benefit pension plans are being put in jeopardy, but there's opportunities here to put the focus on the millions of Canadians that don't have a pension plan and in the importance of the public system. We're engaged in a campaign today along with the other affiliates of the Canadian Labour Congress to put forward a proposal to government where in fact we can strengthen the public pension plan.

Should government be doing something with pension legislation to make sure people get what they paid for?

Government has a fundamental responsibility to play a role in the economy and they just can't abdicate it to the "market". Everything in our lives is regulated, right down to our cats and dogs, and again I can't understand for the life of me how with something as important as the economy, why people feel it should be unregulated and free to do whatever the market dictates as if it is some omnipotent force out there that we can't control. We can control it if we have the political will to do so.

What's a good collective agreement and how do you get that at the bargaining table today?

In a good collective agreement, you address the basic work issues, seniority issues, vacation, benefits, time off the job and have a good remuneration package that allows people to not only subsist but to actually have a life where they can afford a home, afford to put food on the table, afford any additional medical expenses that they would have over and above their benefits and provide their kids with an education.

Where do you see life going for trade unionists and the CAW in the next quarter century?

Unless the system changes, you know, the fights 25 years from now are going to be the same fights that we're engaged in today, which literally are the same fights we were in engaged in 25 years ago. The players change but the fight and the struggle for basic respect in the workplace and for a decent income and being able to build a life with your family in your community, that's been the issue since day one.

Employers, for the most part not individual managers or CEOs but just the nature of capital and how the system operates, are all about limiting that. Everything is interference or a nuisance, an irritant to profit. Profit is not a bad word. For example you have to have profit in order to have investment which provides jobs. But if profit is the only goal, then everything else you do to make life better for the people that are doing the value added, doing the work to provide the profit, is going to cost you a piece of that profit. And as long as that mentality exists, our fight is going to be the same.

Toronto, November 26, 2009

An Interview with

Jean-Pierre Fortin

by Daniel Drolet

Jean-Pierre Fortin has a long history as a trade union activist. As a worker at United Aircraft (now Pratt & Whitney) from 1973 to 1990, he played an active role in the historic 1974 strike. He gradually worked his way up through the union ranks to take on the position of Québec Director of the CAW.

Jean-Pierre Fortin was one of the founding members of the CAW-TCA-Québec Council, on which he served as both vice-president and president. He was also among the officers of the Canadian branch of the United Auto Workers union who decided to break with the UAW in order to found CAW-TCA Canada in 1985. In 1990, he became a CAW national representative, and in this capacity helped to negotiate collective agreements in all sectors. He was elected Québec Director in April 2008, replacing Luc Desnoyers.

Q: What is the path that led you to the labour movement? What values do you identify with the most?

A: I was hired to work at the United Aircraft plant in June 1973, and I had the privilege of joining a department in which my co-worker at the time was the president of the union. So right from the start, I was in direct contact with the union officers in our workplace. And then, January 1974 marked the start of a strike that made history in Québec and Canada – the famous United Aircraft strike that lasted over 20 months. So, I believe that I was privileged to be hired in a department with a strong team of union leaders who were committed activists. I think that that had an enormous influence on my subsequent career choices.

How would you characaterize the political commitment of the CAW?

There is a theme that we are fond of: "CAW Québec – A Different Union" and there are two reasons we use it. One of the fundamental values of our union is that our members, through their delegations in the local unions, have real control over the direction taken by their union. To my knowledge, we are the only union whose leadership meets with the heads of all local unions every six months in order to report on their activities, successes, failures, battles, etc. That means that every six months (through the Québec Council), our members help us identify the priority issues so we can focus on the work that needs to be done.

The Québec Council is really the engine that drives our efforts across the province of Québec; it's where we mobilize our local unions and where we develop our action plans and our programs.

And, secondly, there is the political aspect: in my opinion, we are the most politically engaged union on both the Québec and Canadian stage and that is what sets us apart.

If you had to choose one thing, what has been the Québec Council's greatest contribution to Québec society?

If we take the Québec Council as a whole – that is, the CAW delegation in Québec that's represented by the Québec Council – I would say that our greatest accomplishment is the influence that we've had on the different levels of government in terms of the establishment of social programs.

Times are tough, particularly for workers in the manufacturing sector. How is the CAW dealing with the loss of jobs in manufacturing?

There's no doubt that the union, both in Québec and Canada, is going through an extremely difficult period, because the current crisis has hit the manufacturing industry across the country head-on. These losses have a major impact on us, because there is an important restructuring of the economy going on, with a shift from a production economy to a service economy, and we are extremely concerned.

If you walk around Montréal today, you'll see that the city has an unemployment rate that's above the national average because of the impact of the crisis on the manufacturing industry. On the other hand, there are lots of new hotels being built. This is a sign of the shift to a service economy. And what's worrying about this is that the grassroots that built Canada into a society with good social services and decent wages was based in the manufacturing industry, and less so in the service industry.

So, the question, is how do we deal with this? We've intensified our organizing efforts, the organizing of new members. In Québec, there are a lot of independent unions, and we are working extremely hard to get these small independent unions to join the large CAW family.

The rate of unionization in Québec is roughly 40 per cent, the highest rate in Canada. But that means that 60 per cent of the Québec population does not belong to a union. And out of that 60 per cent, the vast majority are in the service and manufacturing industries. There are tons of small- and medium-sized businesses in Québec that don't have a union. So that's where we're focusing our efforts.

As the proportion of unionized workers in the manufacturing sector declines, will it be more difficult to negotiate good collective agreements?

At every bargaining table we sit down at, employers are taking advantage of the current economic context to extract concessions from the workers we represent.

I would say that here in Québec we have the advantage of a tool that our colleagues elsewhere in the country don't have – I'm referring to the Québec Federation of Labour's Solidarity Fund. In 1984, the

QFL set up a fund to which workers contribute, and today this fund has net assets of nearly $7 billion.

It has become an important economic lever for the province of Québec in that the mission of the fund is to create, maintain and protect jobs and to make strategic investments in Québec businesses. The Solidarity Fund gives us a tool that allows us, when employers demand concessions, to verify whether the company is telling the truth about its situation, because often they're just playing poker with us, or bluffing, when they tell us their company isn't profitable. We are able to determine the real financial situation of the company and once those circumstances have been determined, we can do what needs to be done to save those jobs.

Pension plans are looking very fragile all of a sudden. What should governments do to protect workers' pension plans?

The first thing is double the retirement benefits of workers, from 25 per cent to 50 per cent. Why? Because what we're realizing more and more is that the new generation of workers are likely to change employers more often over the course of their career. And since they'll be working at different places during their career, they won't have time to build up a sufficient retirement fund through a supplemental pension plan.

The public plan, which should cover all workers across the country, should guarantee that we do not live in poverty when we retire, which is not currently the case. And then, afterwards, we can talk about making up for the difference in order to ensure a better income.

Secondly, we need to protect the pension benefits of those who are already retired. We must never forget that these people – who should be taking advantage of their retirement today – are the ones who built the country we live in. If we are able to enjoy the society we live in today, it's thanks to their hard work. Now that they've reached their retirement, it's not acceptable that they have to live with the threat of their pension being cut because the company they worked for is going bankrupt or because of an economic downturn.

I think that governments need to adopt laws that provide a guaranteed income for life to every person who retires across this country, and for that you need legislation.

How can we renew organized labour in Québec in a context where the economy is changing, manufacturing jobs are disappearing and the public sector seems (possibly) to be shrinking?

It is young people who represent the future of organized labour, not only here in Québec, but in the rest of Canada and the world as well. We have to do a better job of reaching out. I have the impression that the young people coming out of our schools and universities have been fed a constant message emphasizing individualistic values and personal success. We need to re-examine our strategies and to improve our capacity to listen to young people and to reach out to them, to offer them services that resonate with them.

The CAW has decided not to automatically support Bloc and PQ candidates. Is it realistic to think that the CAW can support candidates from other parties?

There has, in fact, been a shift within the Québec branch of the CAW as well as at the national level. Historically, since the founding of the Parti Québécois, the Québec branch of the CAW had always supported this party. The same goes for the Bloc Québécois. We systematically supported the Bloc Québécois at the federal level.

But a few years ago, we realized that these political parties took us for granted, so we changed our strategy to make it so that our support has to be earned. Of course, we went through some crises in Québec when the Parti Québécois was in office. This was a party we had supported during the elections, but when times got tough, they acted just like all the other parties and attacked the working class.

Just think back to the 1980s, for example, when the wages of public service employees were slashed by 20 per cent.

And yes, it is possible that, if the parties we traditionally support shift too far to the right and if we can't live with that, as happened at the national level, then we'll decide to vote strategically by backing the candidates who support our union's demands. But in no way does this compromise our political commitment. On the contrary, it reinforces the influence that we can have both on individual Members of Parliament and on the party as a whole.

Montréal, October 27, 2009

On April 23, 2009 15,000 protesters filled the lawn of Queen's Park, Toronto to demand that the Ontario government protect pensions. The huge turnout from unions, retirees' organizations and community groups sent a strong message to governments that people were prepared to fight for social and economic justice for our retirees, present and future.

Right: CAW President Ken Lewenza says the assembled "collective power of people" is there to ensure "working people having the right to retire with dignity and respect, and not having to worry about their pension and retirement income."

Above: CAW retirees listening to Ken Lewenza's speech.

Page 159: Len Harrison, president of the CAW Retired Workers' Advisory Executive at the Queen's Park rally.

The Zellers warehouse strikers lead the CAW delegation in the 2009 Toronto Labour Day parade. Faced with harsh concession demands from their employer, CAW Local 1000 members who work at Zellers warehouse in Toronto took to the picket line July 13, 2009 in a cause adopted by CAW local unions across the country. In support of the striking CAW Local 1000 warehouse workers, many of whom are new Canadians, CAW locals held protests, demonstrations, information pickets and other events from British Columbia to Pointe-Claire, Québec.

Above: Ken Lewenza with the Zellers warehouse workers delegation.

Top left: Bob Orr, assistant to the CAW President, speaks to a demonstration in support of the striking Zellers warehouse workers. *Top right:* Attending the Labour Day parade were also members of the CAW leadership, including Peggy Nash, Jim O'Neil, Peter Kennedy, Jerry Dias, Bob Chernecki, Ken Lewenza, Bob Orr.

Mergers

CAW membership has more than doubled since 1985, as we organize new workers in all sectors of the economy and as smaller unions and employee associations elect to merge under our constitution.

Mergers have diversified and strengthened our membership base, bringing in tens of thousands of new members all across the country.

Following is a list of mergers from 1985 to the present day.

CAW Mergers

Union	Members At Date of Merger	Effective Date
Syndicat des Travailleurs et Travailleuses (cols bleus et cols blanc) de la Mine Niobec	225	March 4, 2008
United Bottlers Workers' Union 9 (ICWU)	117	August 8, 2007
Canadian Racetrack Workers Union (CRWU)	600	March 1, 2007
McMaster University Staff Association (MUSA)	2,700	November 26, 2005
United Bus Workers of Ontario Association, Local 120 (UBWO)	120	March 31, 2005
Syndicat des Travailleurs et Travailleuses en Aeronautique de Longueuil (STTAL)	311	November 16, 2004
Progressive Bakery Workers Association (PBWA)	143	May 5, 2004
Ontario Beverage Workers Union (OBWU)	112	April 6, 2004

Union	Members At Date of Merger	Effective Date
Federation des Syndicats du Secteur Aluminium Inc. (FSSA)	4,600	March 23, 2004
The Canadian Union of Transportation Employees Local 1 (CUTE-Local 1)	140	December 17, 2002
The Canadian Paper Workers Union, Local 219	325	September 16, 2002
Ontario Northland Employees Independent Union (ONEIU)	69	February 3, 2002
The Canadian Air Traffic Control Association (CATCA)	2,200	July 1, 2001
The Air Traffic Specialist Association of Canada (ATSAC)	850	January 1, 2001
Marine Communications and Traffic Services Association (MCTSA)	350	October 22, 2000
Independent Canadian Transit Union, Locals 1 and 2 and	2,950	February 8, 2000
Independent Canadian Transit Union, Local 3	500	August 24, 1998
Retail, Wholesale Canada (RWC)	23,000	November 1, 1999
Ventratech Employees Association	180	March 21, 1999
Marine Workers Federation (MWF)	4,500	August 10, 1996
United Fishermen and Allied Workers Union (UFAWU)	4,500	June 1, 1996

Union	Members At Date of Merger	Effective Date
Quaker Oats Employees Independent Union	400	November 27, 1995
Canadian Seat Assembly Workers Union	525	September 17, 1995
The Newspaper Guild, Local 239 (TNG)	140	August 19, 1995
N & D Supermarket Employees Association	230	April 23, 1995
Canadian Association of Communication and Allied Workers (CACAW)	1,200	February 17, 1995
Independent Canadian Steel Workers Union (ICSWU)	725	August 26, 1994
Canadian Association of Smelter and Allied Workers (CASAW)	2,000	June 2, 1994
Canadian Brotherhood of Railway, Transport and General Workers (CBRT&GW)	33,437	June 1, 1994
Canadian Union of Mine, Mill and Smelter Workers (CUMMSW)	1,600	August 20, 1993
United Electrical, Radio and Machine Workers of Canada (UE)	5,000	September, 1992

Union	Members At Date of Merger	Effective Date
Canadian Textile and Chemical Union (CTCU)	700	June 1, 1992
Canadian Association of Industrial Mechanical and Allied Workers (CAIMAW)	6,500	January 1, 1992
TCU – Airline Division	3,500	May 24, 1990
The Brotherhood of Railway Carmen of Canada	8,000	May 29, 1990
Great Lakes Fishermen and Allied Workers Union (GLFAWU)	400	March 23, 1989
Canadian Seafood and Allied Workers Union (CSAWU)	3,000	May 30, 1989
Fishermen, Food and Allied Workers Union (FFAW)	24,000	November 7, 1988
Canadian Glass Workers Union	800	November 10, 1987
Canadian Association of Passenger Agents (CAPA)	800	January 1, 1987
Canadian Air Line Employees Association (CALEA)	4,100	July 1, 1985
Total Mergers = 40	**145,549**	

Further References

Books

Baruth-Walsh, Mary E. and G. Mark Walsh. *Strike! 99 Days on the Line: The Workers' Own Story of the 1945 Windsor Ford Strike*. Penumbra Press, 1995.

Beck, Kaili and Chris Bowes, Gary Kinsman, Mercedes Steedman, and Peter Suschnigg, in collaboration with Laurentian University, Sudbury, Ontario. *Mine Mill Fights Back: Mine Mill/CAW Local 598 Strike 2000–2001 Sudbury*. Published by Mine Mill/CAW Local 598, 2005.

Gindin, Sam. *The Canadian Auto Workers: The Birth and Transformation of a Union*. Toronto: James Lorimer & Company Ltd., 1995.

Hargrove, Buzz (with Wayne Skene). *Labour of Love: the Fight to Create a More Humane Canada*. Toronto: Macfarlane Walter & Ross, 1998.

Hargrove, Buzz. *Laying it on the Line: Driving A Hard Bargain in Challenging Times*. Toronto: Harper Collins Publishers Ltd., 2009.

Pietropaolo, Vincenzo. Introductory Essay by Sam Gindin. *Canadians at Work*. CAW Canada, 2000. Published in French as *Canadiens au travail*.

Reuther, Victor G. *The Brothers Reuther and the Story of the UAW* (A Memoir). Boston: Houghton Mifflin Company, 1976.

Rinehart, James, Christopher Huxley and David Robertson. *Just Another Car Factory? Lean Production and its Discontents*. Ithaca, New York: ILR Press, 1997.

Roberge, Yvon. *Histoire des TCA au Québec: connaitre le passé pour façonner l'avenir*. Les Editions Fides, 2008.

Sugiman, Pamela. *Labour's Dilemma: The Gender Politics of Auto Workers in Canada, 1937-1979*. Toronto: University of Toronto Press, 1994.

White, Bob. *Hard Bargains: My Life on the Line*. Toronto: McClelland and Stewart, 1987.

Yates, Charlotte A.B. *From Plant to Politics: The Autoworkers Union in Postwar Canada*. Philadelphia: Temple University Press, 1993.

Films, Essays, CD-ROMS, DVDS

Breaking Away: The Formation of the Canadian Auto Workers, essay, written by Sam Gindin. Available on CAW web site.

Caterpillar: The Story of a Plant Closure. Film, Directed by Laszlo Barna and Barry Greenwald; written by Laura Alper. Barna-Alper, 1992.

Final Offer. Film, by Robert Collison and Sturla Gunnarson. National Film Board of Canada, 1985.

Keeping the Promise: the CAW 20 Years Later, 1985-2005. DVD, produced by Real to Reel Productions Inc. for the CAW/TCA Canada, 2005.

Navistar: Promise and Betrayal. Video, produced by Real to Reel Productions Inc. for the CAW/TCA Canada, 2003.

No Power Greater: How Autoworkers in Canada Built a Union and Made History. CD-ROM, researched, written, and designed by the CAW/McMaster History Group: Kathy Bennett, Karen Hadley, Tony Leah, Wayne Lewchuk (McMaster University), Ginette Peters, David Robertson, and Herman Rosenfeld. McMaster University Labour Studies Programme, Hamilton, Ontario, 2003.

No Looking Back. Film, by the Canadian Auto Workers, Barna-Alper Production, 1988.

The Negotiator. Film, directed by Barry Greenwald; written by Barbara Sears. Barna-Alper Production, 1995.

CAW Convention Videos

2009 CAW 9th Constitutional Convention. *Workers in Peril, Union in Action*.

2008 CAW Collective Bargaining & Political Action Convention. *Storm Warnings. Taking on the Challenge*.

2006 CAW 8th Constitutional Convention. *Making a Difference*.

2001 CAW 6th Constitutional Convention. *New Century, Same Struggle*.

1999 CAW Collective Bargaining Convention. *Mobilizing for the New Millenium*.

1997 CAW National Constitutional Convention. *Fighting Back Makes A Difference*.

1995 *Celebrating Ten Years of Social Unionism*. Laszlo Barna Production.

CAW web site: www.caw.ca

Note: Many CAW Locals publish local histories, anniversary books, newsletters and other materials, which can be accessed by contacting the CAW Locals directly.

Acknowledgments

This book is the result of a collective effort, and would not have been possible without the support of many people within the CAW and others.

I would first like to thank the leadership of the CAW for supporting the concept of a visual history to mark the 25th anniversary of the founding of the union: National President Ken Lewenza; Secretary-Treasurer Peter Kennedy; and Québec Director Jean-Pierre Fortin. I would also like to thank the National Executive Board for its support and feedback.

I would also like to acknowledge the members of the previous and now retired CAW leadership of the union, who first approved of the idea for such a book, and entrusted me with the responsibility to carry out this project: former National President Buzz Hargrove; former Secretary-Treasurer Jim O'Neil; and former Québec Director Luc Desnoyers.

I would like to acknowledge Maude Barlow for kindly agreeing to write a foreword; and Randy Ray and Daniel Drolet for their interviews with the leadership.

The idea for the book was first proposed by Jim Paré, retired CAW Communications Director, who also shepherded it through the early concept development and approval stages. With his comprehensive knowledge of the history of the CAW, he has been an essential component of the project.

The CAW Communications Department – Director Shannon Devine; National Representatives John McClyment and Angelo DiCaro; and Support Staff Joan Wright – have been very supportive throughout, and I am particularly appreciative for their feedback and comments as the project developed. I relied on the expertise of Director of Work Organization and Training David Robertson; National Co-ordinator Skilled Trades Union Education Program Tony Leah; National Representative Sue Carter; Librarian Kathy Bennett; Administrative Assistant to the National President Rita Lori; Administrative Assistant to the Québec Director France Tremblay; and Acting Administrative Assistant to the Québec Director Sylvie Bruneau.

In order to locate and retrieve photographs, I am indebted to several CAW Local leaders, staff members, and retired members in locals across the country: Local 444 Public Relations/Managing Editor Gord Gray; Local 222 Communications Director Joe Sarnosvsky; Local 112 President Roland Kiehne; Local 112 *Aircrafter* Editor Nick D'Alicandro; Local 195 *The Standard* Editor Bob Cruise (retired); Local 302 President Nancy McMurphy; Local 2002 President Leslie Dias; Mine Mill Local 598 President Richard Paquin; Local 199 member Mike Gauthier; Local 27 President Tim Carrie; Local 27 Financial Secretary Jim Wilkes; Local 27 Recording Secretary Jim Kennedy; Local 127 President Aaron Neaves; Local 219 Vice-President Marcus Wallace; Local 200 2nd Vice-President Marc Renaud; *The Union Forum* Editor FFAW/CAW Jamie Baker; B.C. Area Director Susan Spratt; International Department Director Annie Labaj; National Representative Gavin McGarrigle; Support Staff New Westminster, B.C. office Sandra Brice; *The Fisherman* Editor Sean Griffin; Local 3000 President Jean Van Vliet; National Representative Susan Burrows; Local 88 President Dan Borthwick; and Local 414 Controller John Hayward . I would also like to thank TCA author Yvon Roberge (retired), and CAW Assistant to the President and author Sam Gindin (retired).

I would like to also thank GM Canada Oshawa and Boeing Canada for their collaboration in facilitating photography of workers in their plants. I am indebted to photographers Murray Mosher, David Hartman, Bill Majesky, Stuart Cryer, Gayle Hurmuses, Roger Enriquez, and Elaine Brière; Bill Moffatt of Avard Productions; Grant Tanabe of Thistle Printing and his staff; and finally, Giuliana Colalillo, my partner.

Vincenzo Pietropaolo

Photo Credits

Every effort has been made to confirm the photographers as listed below. The names of some photographers are not known, and any information to help identify them is welcome.

Baker, Jamie/The Union Forum/FFAW-CAW: 6

Balint, Tom/CAW Local 199: 144 top

Brancaccio, Nick/Union Magazine: 74 bottom

Brière, Elaine: 107

CAW Archives: 99 bottom, 102, 106 top, 115 both, 119 bottom, 124, 125 both, 133 top, 139 top, 143 both, 144 bottom, 146 top and middle, 161 top left

Clark Photographic Ltd.: 52–53

Coornell, Marjanna/CAW Local 4234: 99 top

Courtesy of CAW Local 112: 105 top

Courtesy of CAW Local 2002: 28 both

Courtesy of CAW Local 222: 95 both, 131 bottom

Courtesy of CAW Local 27: 29 both, 49 bottom, 92 bottom, 138 bottom

Courtesy of CAW Local 88: 133 bottom

Courtesy of Jack Nichol Family: 100 top

Cruise, Bob/CAW Local 195: 115 both

Cryer, Stuart: 113 all six

D'Alicandro, Nick/CAW Local 112: 10 top, 118 top, 122–123, 136 top, 145

Enriques, Roger: 76, 77 top right, 77 bottom

Gauthier, Mike/CAW Local 199: 110 both

Gérin-Lajoie, Denyse: 10 bottom

Gray, Gord/Local 444: 136 bottom, 137 both, 138 top, 139 bottom

Griffin, Sean/The Fisherman/UFAWU-CAW: 101 both

Hartman, David: 34–35, 49 top, 50–51, 56 both, 94 both, 109 both

Heller, Ursula: 99 middle

Hurmuses, Gayle: 75 bottom, 79 bottom,

Jones, Monica/TCA-Québec Archives: 108 bottom

Jongué, Serge: 47 top, 108 top

Lalonde, Colin/CAW Local 707: 132 bottom

Majesky, Bill: 54, 55 top left, 55 top right, 83 top, 90, 91, 92 top, 96, 97 both

McCutcheon, Joe /CAW Local 219: 126 bottom

McKenna, T./CAW Archives: 30

Moore, Randy/Windsor Star: 75 top

Mosher, Murray: 20, 22, 23 both, 24 all three, 25 top, 26 top, 37 both, 39 both, 40–41, 42 both, 43, 58–59, 60 both, 61, 62, 78, 79 top, 80–81, 82, 103, 105 bottom, 106 bottom, 119 top, 128 bottom, 134–135, 147 top

Nagy, Arnie/UFAWU-CAW: 100 bottom

Paré, Jim/CAW: 29, 71, 112 bottom

Photographer Unknown/CAW Archives: 26 bottom, 31 top, 32–33, 36, 38, 44 both, 45 both, 48, 55 bottom, 56 bottom, 74 top, 77 top left, 83 bottom, 88–89, 93, 118 bottom, 146 top and middle

Pietropaolo, Vincenzo: 5, 7 bottom, 8 top right, 8 bottom, 9, 11 bottom, 12 top, 13 both, 15, 18, 57 both, 64, 67, 84, 85 both, 86–87, 104 both, 105 both, 128 top, 129, 146 bottom, 147 bottom, 149, 153, 155, 159, 160 both, 161 top right, 161 bottom,

Rooney, Frank/CAW Archives: 25 bottom

Sarnovsky, Joe/CAW Local 222: 120, 121 both, 130 both, 131 top, 132 top left, 132 top right

Smiley, David: 98 all three

TCA-Québec Archives: 46, 47 bottom, 111 both, 116–117

Toronto Star: 31 bottom

Tretiak, Harry and Marie/CAW Local 219: 126 top, 127 both

Webber, George: 8 top left, 12 bottom

Wenk Photography/TCA-Québec Archives: 21

Zimovà, Iva: 7 top, 11 top